STUDIES IN ENGLISH LITERATURE

Volume XVII

JOHN FLETCHER

THE WOMAN'S PRIZE
OR
THE TAMER TAMED

A Critical Edition

by

GEORGE B. FERGUSON
St. Cloud State College

1966

MOUTON & CO.

LONDON · THE HAGUE · PARIS

To G. BLAKEMORE EVANS

CONTENTS

INTRODUCTION

I. CRITICAL APPRAISAL

Critics and editors of Beaumont and Fletcher have traditionally viewed *The Woman's Prize or The Tamer Tamed* as a sequel to or influenced by *The Taming of the Shrew*. Henry Weber and others have indicated that Fletcher's motivating force was to vindicate womanhood from the charges leveled against it in Shakespeare's play and that in order to do so, Fletcher changed the scene to London and had a demure English maiden tame the late Katharina's famous husband. Fletcher may have had some such motives in mind, but it seems more likely that the plot materials of *The Taming of the Shrew* provided him with the basic materials for some interesting speculation. One of Fletcher's favorite devices was to place his characters in a complicated situation and then have them work themselves out of it; *The Taming of the Shrew* might well present such a situation. At the conclusion of Shakespeare's play, the wager among the bride-grooms as to which wife shall prove to be the most docile sees Petruchio winning triumphantly. Katharina has been tamed; she accepts her defeat and has been converted into a model wife, and to all appearances Petruchio and Katharina live happily ever after. Fletcher, however, may well have considered the interesting consequences that would arise if Katharina did not prove to be as docile as the bridegrooms had thought but continued in her shrewish ways until she had made Petruchio a shrew too. If, in addition, Katharina should die after a short period of time, Pe-truchio would be free to marry again. Fletcher could then begin *The Woman's Prize* just after the second marriage and fill in the details necessary to motivate the ensuing action.

Early in the first scene Moroso says:

> What though his other wife,
> Out of her most abundant stubbornes,
> Out of her daily hue and cries upon him,
> (For sure she was a Rebell) turn'd his temper,
> And forc'd him blow as high as she? do'st follow
> He must retain that long since buried Tempest,
> To this soft maid? (I.i.16-22)

Further evidence of the shrewishness of Petruchio's first wife is indicated by Tranio (I.i.25-38), Byanca (I.ii.56-61), and Petruchio (III.iii.151-166). These speeches also indicate that Petruchio was not always as he is now. Tranio says that he is no more the "still Petruchio" since he married his first wife, Maria admits that his first wife set him going, and Petruchio looks to his first doting as a cause of his problems. *The Taming of the Shrew* may be alluded to by Maria's references to Petruchio as a famous woman tamer:

> And I am worse, a woman that can feare
> Neither Petruchio Furius, nor his fame, (I.iii.173-4)

> You have been famous for a woman tamer,
> And beare the fear'd name of a brave wife-breaker: (I.iii.263-4)

Beyond these rather general hints, there is little else to remind the reader of the Shakespeare play except perhaps the Italian names, but only three of them are to be found in *The Taming of the Shrew*. Of these three – Petruchio, Tranio, and Byanca – only Petruchio bears any resemblance to the characters of Shakespeare's play. Tranio, a servant in *The Taming of the Shrew*, is a nobleman and a friend of Petruchio in *The Woman's Prize*. Byanca, the mild sister of Katharina, is cousin to Maria and leader of the rebellion in *The Woman's Prize*. But Fletcher goes no further than this; he repeats none of the speeches, action, or subplotting; instead he turns the plot materials over and transports the action to London – leaving the Italian names and the changed character of Petruchio to hint rather broadly at the older play.

Of lesser importance but perhaps as obvious are the echoes of Aristophanes' *Lysistrata*. Byanca, Maria, and Livia seek an equality with the men, and in order to bring the men to terms, they use what forces they have at their command – they deny the men their love. The women of Greece in Aristophanes' *Lysistrata* brought peace to their various states by denying themselves to their husbands. In *The Woman's Prize* the scenes (II.v,vi) in which the rebellious women debate from their barricaded apartment with Petruchio and his friends in the street below are reminiscent of Lysistrata and the women of Athens as they debate at the gate-way to the Acropolis.

The structure of *The Woman's Prize* consists of two plots – a primary plot involving Petruchio and Maria, and a sub-plot concerning Rowland, Moroso, and Livia. The sub-plot leans on the framework which the primary plot provides; it is so loosely integrated into the play that its lines could, for the most part, be marked out and the play would maintain its structural unity; indeed the eighteenth-century adaptors made the play into an after piece by merely striking out the sub-plot lines and rewriting those few instances where the two plots are woven together. Only three scenes show an integration of the plots; I.i. presents Moroso, Sophocles, and Tranio in a discussion concerning Petruchio's marriage to Maria and Moroso's desire for Livia; I.ii and II.ii provide an opportunity for Livia first to chide Maria and Byanca for their rebellious behavior and later to join them in their barricade. The remainder of the play is composed of scenes alternating between the main plot and the sub-plot with very little attempt at integration.

The sub-plot provides for more comic effect than the main plot, but it is weak in motivation. Livia is in love with young Rowland and detests the rich old Moroso whom her father has selected for her husband. Such a situation is usually worked out by the heroine's finding a way to change her father's wishes; however, Fletcher concentrates on the lovers rather than on the father, and in the denouement Livia tricks Rowland into marrying her, and for no apparent reason Moroso and Petronius are ignored. Such a solution ignores the problem, but it provides for a number of comic scenes in which Livia twits Moroso, misleads Rowland, and allies herself with the other women. Each of these scenes has a unity almost complete within itself, and each adds

to the total effect of the comic element which pervades the play.
The main plot is somewhat better motivated, but it too has its
weaknesses. The conflict involves the equality of the sexes. Maria
has decided to exert her sovereignty, and locks herself in her
apartment until Petruchio will submit to the terms of her demands.
Although she manages to rid him of a fair amount of property
and he appears more docile at the conclusion of the play, he does
not submit to her demands; she merely says that he does, and
this assertion serves as the denouement of the plot:

> I have done my worst, and have my end, forgive me;
> From this houre make me what you please: I have tam'd ye,
> And now am vowd your servant: . . .   (V.vi.44-46)

Neither of the plots contains much rising action in plot structure;
the conflict within the play is never resolved; it merely concludes
after providing the basis for the comic materials.

Whatever *The Woman's Prize* may lack in structure, it makes
up for in comic situation. The prologue, which was obviously
written by someone other than Fletcher since it refers to him in
the third person, calls attention to the comic situation and warns
the audience not to:

> Expect the mazes of a subtle plot
> Set Speeches, high expressions; and what's worse,
> In a true Comedy, politique discourse.

A goodly portion of the comedy thus comes from the situation in
which the characters find themselves. In the opening scene Moroso
finds himself in the embarrassing situation of having to defend
his virility against the onslaught of Sophocles and Tranio, who
know him to be a rich and impotent old man who entertains
thoughts of marrying the attractive young Livia. Later scenes see
the women entrenched against the amorous lovers, Rowland and
Petruchio; Livia taunting Rowland in the presence of Moroso;
Petruchio feigning sickness and getting quarantined for his efforts;
and so on to the conclusion of the play. It is the situation, language, and wit that amuse; the characters, however, are in many
respects Jonsonian humors or the stock characters of Latin
comedy: Rowland, the impetuous young lover; Moroso, the rich

old fool; Petruchio, the impatient husband; Petronius, the ineffective father; Maria, the recalcitrant daughter; Bianca, the trouble maker; etc. The characterizations are simple rather than complex; they are not enigmas to be solved; they are the outlines of people in action – action that is to be laughed at.

In the matter of language, Fletcher is particularly colorful, and *The Woman's Prize* is vividly painted in all the colors and subtle hues. For example, many of the words have a bawdy frankness about them that would have seemed less objectionable to the seventeenth century than they do to the twentieth. Such words as "whore", "maidenhead", "ass", "tail", are forthright terms to be found in the plays of many of Fletcher's contemporaries. Fletcher's real forte lies in the double-entendre and the twisting of an apparently innocent phrase into a suggestive reference:

> *Jaq.* . . . When shall we see your worship run at Ring?
> That houre a standing were worth money.   (I.i.58-59)

> *Petru.* I must not to bed with this stomach, and no meat Lady.
>   (I.iii.221)

> *Row.* . . . Whether goe you?
> *Soph.* To view the works.
> *Row.* What workes?
> *Soph.* The womens Trenches.
> *Row.* Trenches? are such to see?   (I.iv.23-24)

But the bold language of *The Woman's Prize* is by no means restricted to the male characters; the women speak with the same frankness. They talk of whoring, sweating against a cork, placketts, behind kissing, teaching an old stiff jade to trot, backing of dairy maids, and so on through a whole vocabulary of bawdy and semi-bawdy words and phrases. The direct language of the women thus underscores the action of the play. The women are seeking equality and are fighting a man's world; in order to win they must assume their equality and fight force with force. As they see their cause, they can no longer be merely objects to be pursued or pawns to be captured; they must assert their rights and bring the men to a recognition of these rights; thus the action, language, and wit of the men is met with similar action, language, and wit by the women; and the result is one of Fletcher's most comic plays. In order to speak of the position of *The Woman's Prize* in the Beaumont and Fletcher canon, it is necessary to define just what that canon is and what it contains. Such a task is not as uncomplicated as it might seem, for the canon is really the work of Fletcher and his collaborators, with Fletcher as the common element. Thus any complete works of Fletcher include the plays written by Fletcher alone and those written with Beaumont, Massinger, Shakespeare, et al., and although critics have arrived at a generally accepted opinion as to who wrote which plays, the matter is by no means closed. A further complication is that the canon contains a wide variety of plays. It is common to say that Beaumont and Fletcher wrote comedies, tragi-comedies, and tragedies; the names Beaumont and Fletcher are difficult to separate since tradition has bound them so firmly together; and the classification into comedies, tragi-comedies and tragedies is a time honored convenience. But many of the plays are not so easily classified. By its very nature, tragi-comedy is, as it has often been called, the middle genre; it partakes of both tragedy and comedy, and the dividing line between that which is comedy and that which is tragi-comedy is often a matter of varying degree rather than a matter of absolute certainty; *Monsieur Thomas*, for example, has two plots: that involving Thomas and his father is comedy, that concerning Valentine, Francesco, and Callida is tragi-comedy. *The Woman's Prize* presents no such difficulty; no one seriously comes near death; Petruchio's feigned death merely adds to the comic effect of the play, and it is Fletcher's use of these comic materials that most accurately defines the position of *The Woman's Prize* in the Beaumont and Fletcher canon. Sex and the battle of the sexes loom large in the comic elements of Fletcher's plays. In *Monsieur Thomas*, Thomas leads his father, Sebastian, to believe that he has given up his free ways with women and rogues; and Sebastian is astounded and displeased that the family tradition will not be carried on. At the same time, however, Thomas is involved in an affair with Valentine's niece, Mary. The comedy which this conflict provides is in the mode of *The Woman's Prize*.

Oriana's schemes to win back the affections of Mirabel in *The Wild Goose Chase*, and Celia's chastity in *The Humorous Lieutenant* show the further range of Fletcher's use of sex conflict. The list could be extended considerably, and the basic elements would still be present: people placed in a unique and interesting position struggling to get out of their predicament; action that moves the plot at a swift pace and subordinates character development; sex conflicts that produce highly comic scenes; wit that ranges from the forthright obscene to the coarse pun to the double-entendre to the most delicate innuendo. All are a part of Fletcher's comic mode, and all are to be found in *The Woman's Prize*.

II. STAGE HISTORY

Since Professor Maxwell's definitive treatment of the subject in 1935,[1] early 1611 has become the accepted date of composition for *The Woman's Prize*. Professor Maxwell surveys the scholarship which has preceded him concerning the date of the play:

Fleay placed it between 1613 and 1616; Thorndike and Oliphant assigned it to 1603 or 1604; Schelling thought it written "perhaps as early as 1606, if not in 1604"; Lawrence [whose views were unpublished but expressed privately to Oliphant and quoted by him] dated it 1608 and Gayley "*ca.* 1615".

This previous scholarship had relied heavily on the assumption that since *The Woman's Prize* has a direct relationship to *The Taming of the Shrew*, it must be given an early date. Professor Maxwell points out that the earliest date suggested for *The Woman's Prize* is ten years later than the date accepted for the composition of *The Taming of the Shrew*. He further objects to the topical allusion to the siege of Ostend:

The chamber's nothing but a mere Ostend.

(III.iii.88)

Although the siege of Ostend ended September 8, 1604, such an allusion could well have passed into "the realm of figurative language".

Thorndike had held that the mention of the Earl of Tyrone, "These are the most authentique Rebels, next Tyrone, I ever read of" (III.iii. 211), suggested an early date, since Tyrone sub-

[1]   Baldwin Maxwell, "The Woman's Prize, or The Tamer Tamed", *Modern Philology*, XXXII (May, 1935), 353-363.

mitted in 1603 and was in London that summer; however, Maxwell shows that the subsequent career of Tyrone was very much in
the public eye and that in December of 1610 the Privy Council
was investigating a rumour that Tyrone was attempting to incite
a rebellion in Ireland from his exile in Spain.

In II.ii. 66-68 Byanca in referring to Moroso says:

> That everlasting Cassock that has worne
> As many Servants out, as the Northeast passage
> Has consum'd Saylors. . . .

This topical allusion, according to Professor Maxwell, gives evidence for a date of no earlier than 1607 since the only English
attempts to find a Northeast Passage between 1580 and the death
of Fletcher were those carried out by Hudson in 1607, 1608, and
1609. In addition, the allusion seems to suggest that several
attempts have been made and have failed, hence favoring a date
in 1609 or later. The account of Dutch expeditions in the 1590's
was not printed in England until 1609. Hudson's last and most
disasterous voyage was to the northwest, the news of which
reached England in September, 1611; thus an allusion to the
Northeast Passage would not have been likely after this date.

Three more references in the play lead Professor Maxwell to
the composition date of 1611:

> Louder then Tom o'Lincoln   (III.ii.159)

> I never will believe a silent woman   (I.iii.107)

> Contrive you beard o'th top cut like Verdugoes;
> It shows you would be wise, and burn your night-cap,
> It looks like halfe a winding-sheet   (IV.i.55-57)

The first of these most likely refers to the recasting and rehanging
of the great bell in Lincoln Cathedral in December of 1610; [2] the
last two may refer to Jonson's *Silent Woman* (1609) and *The
Alchemist* (1610) respectively; thus the most convincing evidence
points to a date of early 1611 for *The Woman's Prize*, and recent
scholarship accepts this date.[3]

If the matter of the date of *The Woman's Prize* has occasioned

[2] See Critical Note III.iii.159 (p. 214).
[3] Clifford Leech, *The John Fletcher Plays* (Cambridge, 1962), p. 50.

diverse opinion, the matter of authorship has been decisively in favor of Fletcher as the sole author; however, the tests or methods used to establish Fletcher's characteristics are by no means as absolute or definitive as one might wish. All who have attempted the setting up of a series of criteria for testing authorship in the Beaumont and Fletcher canon have expressed their reservation as to the perfection of their methods or results. From Oliphant to Hoy, the method has been to find that play or plays that are unquestionably by a certain author, delineate that author's salient characteristics, and use those characteristics as the touchstone for identifying that author's hand elsewhere.

In the matter of the Beaumont and Fletcher materials, scholars are satisfied that by using this method they can, with reasonable certainty, identify those portions which belong to Beaumont and Fletcher's collaborators. Separating the hand of Beaumont from that of Fletcher is based on much less certainty. Fletcher's autograph is found in only one place: in a letter, written for him by a scribe, to the Countess of Huntington, he makes corrections and attaches his signature and address; but very little can be deduced from this evidence.

The Faithful Shepherdess is the only play which can with a great degree of certainty be said to be wholly Fletcher's, and it is from this play that scholars have sought the keys for identifying Fletcher's part in the other works of the canon. Professor Hoy, however, discounts the value of *The Faithful Shepherdess* in respect to linguistic keys since it is a pastoral and abounds naturally in archaic forms which are not typically Fletcherian. Professor Hoy's method is to show the linguistic peculiarities which fourteen of the plays (including *The Woman's Prize*) in the canon uniquely have in common and then to point out that these plays could not have been written by Fletcher's collaborators; thus they must belong to Flecher.[4]

The keys which the scholars have found, are for the most part, a series of versification and linguistic peculiarities based on the texts of the printed editions, and even a hurried look at these

---

[4]   Cyrus Hoy, "Fletcher and His Collaborators", *Studies in Bibliography*, ed. by Fredson Bowers (Charlottesville, 1956), VIII, 132-142.

editions shows a wide diversity of opinion concerning versification and lineation. Only five seventeenth-century manuscripts of the plays which appear in the first folio (1647) are extant: *Bonduca* (Additional MS. 36758 in the British Museum), *Demetrius and Enanthe* – printed in the folio under the title *The Humorous Lieutenant* (Brogyntyn MS. 42 in the library of Lord Harlech), *The Honest Mans Fortune* (Dyce MS. 9), *The Beggars Bush* (Lambarde MS. in the Folger Library), and *The Woman's Prize* (Lambarde MS. in the Folger Library). Three other Beaumont and Fletcher plays exist in manuscript: *The Elder Brother* (MS. Eg. 1994 in the British Museum), *The Faithfull Friends* (Dyce MS. 10), and *Sir John van Olden Barnavelt* (Additional MS. 18653 in the British Museum). An exhaustive study of these manuscripts, the quartos, folios, and later additions would undoubtedly provide new information as to the style of Fletcher and his collaborators. Until such is done, one must – with caution – use the evidence that is now available.

The Woman's Prize contains most of the characteristics traditionally ascribed to Fletcher's style. Most of the lines are end-stopped; only occasionally does one find enjambement, and rhyme occurs only when a character quotes a line from a song or a poem. Dactyls and anapests are freely used as substitute feet, and in a number of instances a foot is three or four syllables in length; thus there are some lines that are thirteen or more syllables long. The line endings are of particular interest since many have two stresses and a few have three; in addition there are lines that are basically iambic, eleven syllables long, and the tenth and eleventh syllables are accented: "Out of her daily hue and cries upon him", I.i.18. The use of feminine endings in *The Woman's Prize* is quite frequent,[5] but as Professor Oliphant points out, weak endings are "by no means common"[6] in Fletcher's lines.

As Professor Bald indicates, certain colloquial forms and ab-

---

[5] Exceeding harshly, and not like a Father, I.i.6.
To please the father for his second daughter. I.i.11.
(For sure she was a Rebell) turn'd his temper, I.i.19.
And forc'd him blow as high as she? do'st follow I.i.20.
He must retain that long since buried Tempest, I.i.21.

[6] E. H. C. Oliphant, *The Plays of Beamont and Fletcher*, p. 34.

breviations are thought to distinguish Fletcher's work from that of others.[7] Chief among these is said to be Fletcher's preference of "ye" for "you", and Professor Hoy assigns *The Woman's Prize* wholly to Fletcher primarily on the basis of this evidence.[8] The Lambarde manuscript does show this preference to a greater degree than the first folio, which has "ye" a total of eighty-four times. The manuscript has "ye" eighty-five times where the first folio has "you", and "you" only eighteen times where the first folio has "ye". In the matter of the other colloquialisms and the abbreviations the evidence is too scanty to have any significance.

Thus the scholarship and whatever internal evidence there is point to John Fletcher as having written *The Woman's Prize* and to the date of composition as the early part of 1611.

The original production of *The Woman's Prize* was probably licensed by George Buck, but the 1633 revival by the King's Men occasioned Sir Henry Herbert, then Master of the Revels, to issue a warrant suppressing the performance of the play. Herbert records in his office book the circumstances surrounding this incident.

On friday the nineteenth [later he refers to the date as the eighteenth] of October, 1633, I sent a warrant by a messenger of the chamber to suppress *The Tamer Tamd*, to the Kings players, for that afternoone, and it was obeyd; upon complaints of foule and offensive matters conteyned therein.
They acted *The Scornful Lady* instead of it; I have enterd the warrant here:
These are to will and require you to forbeare the actinge of your play called *The Tamer Tamd, or the Taminge of the Tamer*, this afternoone, or any more till you have leave from mee: and this at your perill. On friday morninge the 18 Octob. 1633.
To Mr. Taylor, Mr. Lowins, or any of the King's players at the Blackfryers.
On saterday morninge followinge the booke was brought mee, and at my lord of Hollands request I returned it to the players ye monday morninge after, purgd of oaths, prophaness, and ribaldrye, being ye 21 of Octob. 1633.

[7]   R. C. Bald, *Bibliographical Studies in the Beaumont & Fletcher Folio of 1647*, p. 99.
[8]   Hoy, p. 140.

Because the stoppinge of the acting of this play for that afternoone, it being an ould play, hath raysed some discourse in the players, thogh no disobedience, I have thought fitt to insert here ther submission upon a former disobedience. [Here he inserts the submission of the players in 1624 when they had performed Massinger's *Spanish Viceroy* without his permission.]

All ould plays ought to bee brought to the Master of the Revells, and have his allowance to them, for which he should have his fee, since they may be full of offensive things against church and state; ye rather that in former time the poetts tooke greater liberty than is allowed them by mee.

The 24 Octob. 1633, Lowins and Swanston were sorry for their ill manners, and craved my pardon, which I gave them in presence of Mr. Taylor and Mr. Benfeilde.[9]

When Herbert returned the manuscript to the King's Men, he attached a letter to Knight, their bookkeeper:

Mr. Knight,

In many things you have saved mee labour; yet wher your judgment or penn fayld you, I have made boulde to use mine. Purge ther parts, as I have the booke. And I hope every hearer and player will thinke that I have done God servise, and the quality no wronge; who hath no greater enemies than oaths, prophaness, and publique ribaldry, whch for the future I doe absolutely forbid to bee presented unto mee in any playbooke, as you will answer it at your perill   21 Octob. 1633.[10]

The extent to which the play was censored will be treated below; let it suffice here to note that the King's Men must have produced the play since they went to the trouble of having it examined by Herbert. According to Malone's *Shakespeare* by Boswell, it was acted before the King and Queen at St. James November 28, 1633,[11] and is listed among the plays acted by Red-Bull actors shortly after the Restoration.[12]

That the play was produced as an afterpiece in 1760 is attested to by Richard Owen Cambridge, who wrote an epilogue for the occasion.[13] But more convincing evidence of its popularity in the eighteenth century is the existence of two manuscript

---

[9] J. Q. Adams, *Dramatic Records of Sir Henry Herbert,* pp. 20-21.
[10] Adams, p. 21.
[11] Vol. III, p. 234.
[12] Vol. III, p. 272.
[13] *Works,* p. 314.

versions: the Larpent manuscript in the Huntington Library and the U. of I. manuscript in the library of the University of Illinois.

The Larpent MS contains a note dated 1757 and signed by D. Garrick:

S^r. This Farce we intend to have performed at our Theatre if it meets
with the approbation of my L^d. Chamberlain
from y^r. humble
Servt. D. Garrick
Ap: 25th.
1757.

However, the play is not in his hand but in the same hand as the U. of I. MS; thus both would appear to be closely related in a number of respects. Both have eliminated the sub-plot concerning Rowland, Livia, and Moroso; and cut the play to three acts. Both are cut versions of the play rather than adaptations of the plot materials; most of the lines still contain Fletcher's words, but the lines have been made regular and basically iambic pentameter. The elimination of the sub-plot has necessitated the reassigning of some of the lines, and the manuscripts are in complete agreement in their assigning of speech prefixes. The manuscripts differ in that the Larpent MS gives a more complete version since it has about sixty-five lines which the U. of I. MS lacks, but it omits ten words and two-and-a-half lines found in the U. of I. MS. These variants appear to be simply the result of two cuttings of the play rather than the elimination of some offensive matter.

The U. of I. MS is a theatrical copy which has been annotated and revised by two separate hands. In one instance a line, which was originally omitted, has been added from the version in the Larpent MS by one of these revisers, but for the most part the revisers limited themselves to crossing out lines, adding stage directions, and indicating the side for entrances and exits.

The source which lies behind these revisions is obscured by the fact that the lines which show variants among the two folios and 1711 are omitted, and Sympson's edition with its interesting lineation and meter seems to have been ignored.

III. THE TEXTS AND THE LAMBARDE
MANUSCRIPT

Three seventeenth-century texts of *The Woman's Prize* are extant; these include the first folio of 1647 (F1), the second folio of 1679 (F2), and a manuscript in the Lambarde collection in the Folger Library (MS). At first glance it would appear that these form an ancestral series in the order MS, F1, F2; but there is very little external evidence to support such a view. F1 was certainly available to the editors of F2, and both claim to be based on "the authors' original copies". The relationship between the two is very close; each contains a number of misreadings and typographical errors – some of these they share in common, and some are unique to one or the other of them. F2, however, uniquely contains a song at II.vi.44 – which the title page says has been added to the original copies – and a list of dramatis personae. The greatest number of variants is in the accidentals (spelling and punctuation) and in the lineation, but a number of substantive variants also occur. Perhaps most significant is the three maids scene which F1 erroneously inserts as II.iii. and repeats in its correct position, at the conclusion of act V. F2 gives the scene only once but in the wrong place. Another significant variant occurs at II.iii.4. F1 erroneously reads, "*Row*. Thou hast heard I am sure of Esculapius" and repeats the line again in its correct position ten lines later; F2 in this instance has the reading in the correct position only. See Critical Notes II.iii.4. (p. 208).

MS provides a number of substantive readings which are to be found in none of the other texts; in addition it varies markedly from the folios in the matter of accidentals, but tends to agree more often with F2 than with F1. This problem will be treated later; the matter to be treated here is the rationale of the copy-text, and since it is difficult to establish with any certainty an ancestral series and thus use the earliest extant text as copy-text, F1 – the first printed edition – was chosen as the copy-text for the present edition. The authority for this is based on the advice of W. W. Greg:

... when there is more than one substantive text of comparable authority, then although it will ... be necessary to choose one of them as copy-text, and to follow it in accidentals, this copy-text, can be allowed no over-riding or even preponderant authority so far as substantive readings are concerned. The choice between these, in cases of variation, will be determined partly by the opinion the editor may form respecting the nature of the copy from which each substantive edition was printed, which is a matter of external authority; partly by the intrinsic authority of the several texts as judged by the relative frequency of manifest errors therein; and partly by the editor's judgement of the intrinsic claims of individual readings to originality – in other words their intrinsic merit, so long as by 'merit' we mean the likelihood of their being what the author wrote rather than their appeal to the individual taste of the editor.[14]

In establishing the copy-text, five copies of F1 were collated to discover press-variant formes. Four of these copies are in the University of Illinois library and are catalogued as Copy No. 1, Copy No. 2, Copy No. 3, and Copy No. 4; the fifth copy was loaned to the editor by Professor T. W. Baldwin from his personal library. The collation revealed no press-variant formes.

Professor Bald – by identifying the blocks, ornamental letters, and other typographical material used in F1 – concluded that the section containing *The Woman's Prize* was printed by Edward Griffin [15] and that only one compositor set the type for the play.[16] Professor Gerritsen's re-investigation confirms Professor Bald's conclusions.[17]

The editions of *The Woman's Prize* that appeared after the seventeenth century form an ancestral series that reflects the

[14] "The Rationale of Copy-text", *Studies in Bibliography*, III (1950-51), 29.
[15] Bald, pp. 16-17.
[16] Bald, pp. 20-21.
[17] Johan Gerritsen, "The Printing of the Beaumont and Fletcher Folio", *The Library*, Fifth Series, III (March, 1949), 233-234.

spelling and punctuation of their publication date. The first of these was the seven volume edition of 1711. The volumes are numbered consecutively and *The Woman's Prize* is found in volume six, pages 2914 to 3004. It is an octavo with an illustration opposite the title page of each play. The illustration for *The Woman's Prize* is a stylized picture of Petronius, Sophocles, Moroso, and Maria elaborately dressed in eighteenth-century costumes and standing around the coffin of Petruchio in an eighteenth-century drawing room. A collation of this text with its predecessors shows it to be a direct copy of F2 with no real attempt to correct the errors of its copy-text, adding a goodly share of misreadings and typographical errors of its own.

On 1750 Theobald, Seward, and Sympson published *The Works of Mr. Francis Beaumont and Mr. John Fletcher.* Theobald had planned to do the complete edition, but he died after having completed only the first volume and part of the second; the completion of the work then fell to Seward and Sympson. Volume eight contains *The Woman's Prize*, pages 169-267, and is the work of Sympson with occasional references in the critical notes to the opinions of Seward. This edition is probably the most unsatisfactory of any of the Beaumont and Fletcher editions. Their copy-text was most likely the 1711 edition [18] although they maintained in the title-page that their text had been "collated with all the former editions". The greatest weakness of this edition is the lineation since the editors were determined at all costs to make the lines pentameters. This determination led them to chopping off lines at the end of every tenth syllable, forcing lines to meet their requirements by eliding syllables, and adding words to make the lines longer. Their critical notes are often inadequate or misleading, and in several instances they lack the courage of their convictions; they discuss what should be the correct reading but allow their text to stand in error.

George Colman edited an illustrated edition of *The Dramatic Works of Beaumont and Fletcher* in ten volumes in 1778. *The Woman's Prize* occupies volume eight, pages 274 to 380. This

---

[18]   A collation between Sympson's text and F1, F2, and 1711 shows an overwhelming agreement of Sympson's text with 1711.

edition is a more fortunate one than Sympson's, since he tried to correct the errors of the former editions and used F2 as his copy-text. His sparse notes, however, are heavily indebted to J. Monck Mason's *Comments on the Plays of Beaumont and Fletcher.* The Colman edition was evidently a popular one since it was reprinted in 1811.

The best edited edition up to its time is Henry Weber's *The Works of Beaumont and Fletcher in Fourteen Volumes,* issued in 1812. *The Woman's Prize* is in volume five, pages 251-400. Weber appears to have chosen F1 as his copy-text [19] and claims to have collated all subsequent editions to it; however, the work evidences that his collation was not as complete as it should have been. He makes use of J. Monck Mason's notes (1798), fills in blank spaces in the early texts, and silently adds stage directions and settings for the scenes, but his critical judgment was sound enough to be copiously copied by Alexander Dyce, who is generally considered to have produced the most definitive edition of Beaumont and Fletcher.

In 1840 George Darley edited *The Works of Beaumont and Fletcher,* but this two-volume edition is merely a reprint of Weber's text and notes.

The Reverend Alexander Dyce's eleven volume edition, 1843-6, is generally considered to be the most complete and authoritative text of the Beaumont and Fletcher canon. *The Woman's Prize* is in volume seven, pages 95 to 210. His collation of the early folios produced a fairly valid text based on F1, and his notes incorporated the best of the previous editors, J. Monck Mason, and the unpublished notes of Benjamin Heath. Dyce, however, did not hesitate to supply words for the long dashes which occur in the early folios; a number of his substitutions are incorrect, and he makes substitutions many times where the author was using a dash to indicate an interruption of the speech by another character, and the edition has copious stage directions which he borrowed from Weber and expanded.

---

[19]   Weber says that he chose the earliest printed text as his copy-text, and a collation of his text with the earlier editions bears out the truth of his statement as far as is possible.

From 1905 to 1912 A. R. Waller and E. A. Glover edited *The Works of Francis Beaumont and John Fletcher* in ten volumes. *The Woman's Prize* is the first play in volume ten, edited by Waller. The copy-text for this edition is F2, and a brief collation with F1 and with other early seventeenth century editions, if there were any, is provided at the end of each volume, but there are no critical notes. Since *The Woman's Prize* has never been anthologized and since the uncompleted variorum edition, 1904-12, under the general editorship of A. H. Bullen, does not contain *The Woman's Prize*, the Glover-Waller edition has value in that it makes otherwise unobtainable copies of the plays available to students, but it adds little that is new to the textual study of Beaumont and Fletcher.

At the W. G. Lambarde sale in London, 18 June 1924, item number 528 was a bound volume of manuscripts from the Lambarde family library at Sevenoaks, Kent. The volume contained the manuscripts of five plays: *The Inconstant Lady, The Woman's Prize, The Lost Lady, The Beggars Bush*, and *Hengist*; and fragments of *The Lovers Hospitall*. This volume, known as the Lambarde Volume or the Lambarde Collection of Plays, was purchased by a Major Barrett. H. C. Folger obtained it from Frank Marcham in 1925, and it subsequently became a part of the holdings of the Folger Shakespeare Library in Washington, D.C.

According to the records of G. E. Dawson, who supervised the separate rebinding of the plays in the volume in 1956, the volume was bound in sprinkled calf of *ca.* 1725, sewn on five bands, the backstrip elaborately decorated in the style of the period. The backstrip was much decayed, and both boards were detached. All edges of the leaves were sprinkled with red.

In 1956 the directors of The Folger Library decided to take the volume apart and bind the various plays separately. The care with which this was done is recorded by Mr. Dawson in a letter bound with the manuscript of *The Inconstant Lady*:

I myself [Dawson] assisted in taking it apart and can assert with confidence that the greatest care was used to retain all leaves in their original order and as nearly as possible in their original state and to record all evidence that might throw any light on the past history of the MSS – especially such evidence as would be obscured or destroyed in rebinding.

The Woman's Prize, The Lovers Hospitall, and *The Beggars Bush* did not have stab holes, a condition that indicates that they had "remained loose or been previously bound before being bound in the Lambarde volume". Before the volume was taken apart the versio side of each page was numbered consecutively with the exception of the first two flyleaves, which are blank except for some old shelf numbering. *The Woman's Prize* was the third play in the volume; the first play had been previously cut out of the volume and only the stubs of the folios remained; the second play, *The Inconstant Lady,* was numbered through folio 68; Folios 69 and 70 were two leaves from *The Lovers Hospitall.* Folios 71 through 121 (101 pages 30 by 20 cm.) contained *The Woman's Prize:*

Folios 71-74   A quire of two sheets: 71:74; 72:73.
        75-82   A quire of 4 sheets: 75:82, 76:81, etc. When the heavy glue was removed and these leaves were taken apart 75:82 were not actually conjugate, but there was every indication that they had been. All other pairs were conjugate.
        83-86   A quire of 2 sheets: 83:86, 84:85.
          87   A single leaf without a stub, no gap in text.
        88-93   A quire of 3 sheets: 88:93, 89:92, 90:91.
        94-99   A quire of 3 sheets: 94:99, 95:98, 96:97.
    100-105   A similar quire of six ff.
    106-111   A similar quire of 6 ff.
    112-117   A similar quire of 6 ff.
    118-121   A quire of 2 sheets: 118-121, 119:120.

Folios 122-157 were *The Lost Lady;* 158-204 *The Beggars Bush;* 205-250 *Hengist.* "Then follow 33 stubs from which had been rudely slashed leaves of *The Lovers Hospitall.*"

The manuscript of *The Woman's Prize* (MS) has no title page; however, the top of the first page contains the following heading in a modern hand:

This is a manuscript of Beaumont & Fletcher's
Comedy entitled – The Woman's Prize, or The Tamer Tam'd. – Vol. 6

With the exception of the designation of the second scene in act one, MS provides designations for the acts but not for the scenes and is a shorter version of the play than the text in F1-2. It omits the prologue, epilogue, persons of the play, two complete scenes – II.i and IV.i, the song in act two – although traces of fiber embedded in sealing wax indicate a song may at one time have been attached there – and all references to the Doctor and Pothecary – III.v.55-64. The omission of the scenes and the reference to the Doctor and Pothecary indicate that the text behind MS was probably a shortened, acting version of the play. MS stage directions, for the most part, are more complete and give credence to the view that it is based on a performance text since they occur earlier in MS than they do in F1-2. In one instance MS stage direction, in the same hand as the text, is designated twice so that the difficult entrance clue will not be missed:

Enter   Not certaine neither, what a hap had I? – Enter Maria.
Maria   / & what a tydie. . . .

F1-2 at V.i.68 reads:

Enter Livia discovered abed, and Moroso by her.
By. Pray draw 'em softly, ...

but MS reads:

Enter Liuia sick carryed in a chaire by seruants; Moroso by her.
By. Pray beare her softly, ...

and omits "draw all the Curtaines close" at line 156. It is evident that the folios represent a text which used a bed whereas MS substitutes a chair. Professor Bald hints that the original text called for a bed but that the exigencies of the theatre compelled the use of a chair.[20] Such revisions of the text would not argue for the priority of any of the seventeenth-century texts but would lend weight to the supposition that three different historical circumstances lie behind MS, F1, and F2 respectively.

The variant readings, which a collation of MS, F1 and F2

[20]   Bald, p. 78.

reveals, give ample proof that MS is not a copy of the folio texts; and although it cannot be proved that the actual copy of MS was made before the publication of F1 in 1647, it is evident that the copy-text behind MS is a substantive text.

MS is written in a very clear italic hand which avoids the use of the long s. Professor Bald says: "The complete absence of the long s is particularly noticeable." [21] Actually the long s is rarely used in MS, but it does occur twenty-seven times. Bald is probably correct in stating that the spelling belongs to the first half of the seventeenth century, and the italic hand, though comparatively rarely met with, was taught in the first half of the seventeenth century.[22] And, since the prologue and epilogue were written for the 1633 revival of play, their absence in MS might be taken to suggest that MS represents a text of the play prior to this revival. The fact that the Lambarde volume was in a late seventeenth-century binding when it was purchased by H. C. Folger and the fact that *The Woman's Prize* evidences having been bound earlier indicate that MS *could* date from the early part of the century; in addition, MS shows corrections which were made later by another scribe in a definite seventeenth-century, secretary hand:

That ever yet was chronicl'd] the line originally read, "that yet ever was chronicl'd" but was corrected by crossing out "yet" and inserting it in its proper place by means of a caret. (II.vi.90)

And brave ones too; My hood shal] "hood" was omitted and corrected by a caret. (II.vi.95)

recreant] original scribe wrote "recant" which was crossed out and corrected by the later scribe. (II.vi.104)

Other similar corrections are to be found in IV.ii.37,59.

Henry Herbert's Office Record Book reveals that he censored *The Woman's Prize* in 1633, but the copy-text of MS was either not the text which Herbert censored or if it was, the scribe succeeded in restoring much of it to its original state – a task which the F1-2 editors were unable or unwilling to accomplish. The majority of the substantive readings which MS restores to the

[21]   Bald, p. 51.
[22]   Bald, p. 51.

text come under what Herbert called "oaths, prophaness", and "obsceanes".[23] Just what he considered to be prophaness and obsceanes is a bit difficult to discover, but he records in his office book under the date 9 January 1633, a discussion which he had with King Charles I concerning oaths:

> The kinge is pleased to take *faith, death, slight*, for asservations, and no oaths, to which I doe humbly submit as my masters judgment; but, under favour, conceive them to be oaths, and enter them here, to declare my opinion and submission.[24]

"Faith" used as an oath occurs six times in MS where the folios have a dash or a substitute such as "word" or "well". MS has "death" three times while the folios have "why" or a dash; however, "slight" is used in neither MS nor the folios, and MS shows a definite aversion to the use of "God" most regularly substituting "heaven" in place of it. In other instances MS has "Birlady" for the folios' "Indeed", "heavens" for "honours", "a Christian feare" for "a certain feare", and "yor faith" for "your word". In a number of other instances the folios reveal the censor's work by providing dashes for the obliterated words while MS supplies text:

> by— F1-2; by this hand MS (II.iv.5)
> A— on't F1-2; O Pox on't MS (III.i.47)
> its— F1; it's— F2; rots take me. MS (III.iii.143)

In the matter of obscenities, MS supplies a number of readings which would most certainly have been objectionable:

> pisse] MS; unready F1 * (I.i.46)
> *Row.* I had rather feele it] MS; *om.* F1 * (I.ii.52)
> *Sopho.* His warlike launce
>   Bent like a crosse bow lath, alas the while] MS;
>   *om.* F1 * (I.iii.21-22)
>
> . . . her plackett
> Lookes like the straights of Gibraltar, still wider
> Downe to the gulphe, all sun-burnt Barbary
> Lyes in her breech] MS; *om.* F1 * (II.iv.45-48)
> To turn my tooles to?] MS; To turn my love to F1 * (III.iii.53)
> pispots.] MS; looking-glasses F1 * (IV.ii.2)

23   Adams, p. 19.
24   Adams, p. 22.

A number of other variants, which are to be found only in MS, are what Herbert would have called profanities or material offensive to the church:

Tran.   That anie privie S^t. even small S^t. Davy
   May lash him with a leeke. MS; *om.* F1 * (I.iii.24-25)
   . . . against the Cannons
   Of two church-wardens, made it good, and fought 'em
   & in the churchyard after even song. MS;
   . . . against the Cannons
   Of the town, made it good, and fought 'em
   F1 *   (II.iv.69-71)
Tran.   Of what religion are they,
Row.   Good old Catholikes,
   They deale by intercession all, they keepe
   A kind of household Gods, call'd chamber-maides,
   Which being pray'd to, and their offerings brought,
   (W.^{ch} are in gold, yet some observe the old law
   And give 'em flesh) probatum est, you shall have
   As good love for your monie, and as tydie
   As ere you turn'd your legge ore, and that ended MS;
   om. F1 *   (III.i.50-57)

On the other hand, MS shows evidence of having been copied from a text which had also undergone cutting of some type. The most significant evidence of deletion is the blank space about six lines long at II.iii.33. The lines in MS copy-text were most likely crossed out so that the scribe could not readily read them; he thus left the place for them blank in the expectation of returning to them later and deciphering them.[25]

In addition to supplying readings which no other text contains, MS corrects errors in the folio texts from time to time, provides a check against the emendations that editors have made in the folio texts, and gives evidence for establishing a more faithful text than has hitherto been possible.

The matter of the lineation of the text has been a particularly bothersome problem since none of the extant texts, with the exception of those printed in the variorum edition, have been numbered. In respect to *The Woman's Prize,* the editors either followed

[25]   Bald, p. 18.

the lineation of one of the folios or broke the lines as they saw fit. Both of these procedures have their limitations. The compositors of the folios were restricted to a line of about fifty-five ems, and although they seem to have made a conscientious attempt to follow their copy-text by justifying the lines to fit the space provided – even to the extent of allowing the line to spill over above or below, many of the lines were so long that they had to be split into two short lines. Thus the lineation of the folios is in many instances the result of the compositor's necessity and in some instances his fancy. Some editors, most notably Theobald, Seward, and Sympson, insisted on pentameter lines and relying on their general distrust of compositors and printers, broke the lines as they saw fit. Unfortunately their understanding of Fletcher's metrics left much to be desired and produced a corrupt text.

The size of the sheets in MS imposed no physical restrictions on the scribe in respect to the length of the lines. The left margins are a quarter of a page in width and contain the speech prefixes; the right margins contain most of the stage directions, and, in almost every instance, are large enough to have accommodated much longer lines if they had been required. It seems likely that the scribe of MS tried to reproduce the lines as he found them in his copy-text. At I.ii.95 the MS copy-text most likely read: "thy offerings to protract, and to keepe / fasting my valiant Bridegroome." The scribe when he came to write these lines forgot that the first line ends with "keepe" and began to write "fasting" after "keepe", but he noticed his mistake after writing the first letter; thus MS reads, ". . . and to keep f / fasting . . ." Since MS offers the best rationale for lineation and since the lineation of MS is in accord with what is generally accepted as Fletcher's metrical pattern, this edition follows the lineation of MS except where an emendation or some other consideration makes the practice impossible.

IV. EDITORIAL PROCEDURE

All substantive and semi-substantive changes in the copy-text are recorded in a note at the bottom of the text-page itself. Only the immediate source of the emendation is recorded here since later editors' readings appear in the Historical Collation. The rejected reading of the copy-text is recorded for all contemporary editions. The following sigla are used:

MS   Lambarde Manuscript
F1   First folio (1647)
F2   Second folio (1679)
1711   1711 illustrated, octavo edition
Sympson   Theobald, Seward, Sympson edition (1750)
Colman   George Colman edition (1778)
Weber   Henry Weber edition (1812)
Dyce   Alexander Dyce edition (1845)
Waller   A. R. Waller and E. A. Glover edition (1912)
Mason   J. Monck Mason, *Comments on the Plays of Beaumont and Fletcher* (1798)
Heath   The unpublished notes of Benjamin Heath
*   And all subsequent editions not previously mentioned.

The list of Emendations of Accidentals contains all alterations in the copy-text in respect to the matters of spelling, italics, word division, line division, and punctuation which is neither substantive nor semi-substantive.

The Historical Collation records the substantive and semi-substantive readings of all later editions, contemporary and edited, and repeats the information in the text-footnotes where there is other information to be recorded for later texts not already included in the text-footnote.

The only silent corrections made in the copy-text occur when the text is emended from MS. In this case "u" is normalized to "v" and the beginning of each line is capitalized in order to make the passage conform to the nature of the copy-text.

THE
WOMAN'S PRIZE:
OR,
The Tamer Tamed.

A Comedy.

THE PERSONS REPRESENTED IN THE PLAY

Men.

Moroso, *an old rich doating Citizen, suitor to Livia.*

Sophocles,
Tranio, } *Two Gentlemen, friends to Petruchio.*   5

Petruchio, *An Italian Gent. Husband to Maria.*

Rowland, *A young Gent. in love with Livia.*

Petronius, *Father to Maria and Livia.*

Jaques,
Pedro, } *Two witty servants to Petruchio.*   10

Doctor,

Apothecarie,

Watchmen,

Porters,

Women.   15

Maria, *A chaste witty Lady,* } *The two masculine daughters*
Livia, *Mistress to Rowland.* } *of Petronius.*

Biancha, *Their Cosin, and Commander in chief.*

City Wives,
Countrey Wives, } *To the relief of the Ladies, of which,*
Maids. *two were drunk.*   20

The Scene London.

PROLOGUE

Ladies to you, in whose defence and right,
    Fletchers *brave Muse prepar'd herself to fight*
A battaile without blood, 'twas well fought too,
    (The victory's yours, though got with much ado.)
We do present this Comedy, in which   5
    A rivulet of pure wit flowes, strong and rich
In Fancy, Language, and all parts that may
    Adde grace and ornament to a merry Play.
Which this may prove. Yet not to go too far
    In promises from this our female war,   10
We do intreat the angry men would not
    Expect the mazes of a subtle plot,
Set Speeches, high expressions; and what's worse,
    In a true Comedy, politique discourse.
The end we ayme at, is to make you sport;   15
    Yet neither gall the City, nor the Court.
Heare, and observe his Comique straine and when
    Y're sick of melancholy, see't agen.
'Tis no deere Physick, since 'twill quit the cost:
    Or his intentions, with our pains, are lost.   20

Enter Moroso, Sophocles, and Tranio, with Rosemary,
as from a wedding

Moroso. God give 'em joy.
Tra.   Amen.
Soph.   Amen, say I too:
The Pudding's now i'th proof; alas poor wench,
Through what a mine of patience must thou worke,
Ere thou know'st good houre more?
Tra.   Tis too true: Certaine,
Methinks her father has dealt harshly with her,   5
Exceeding harshly, and not like a Father,
To match her to this Dragon; I protest
I pity the poore Gentlewoman.
Mor.   Me thinks now,
He's not so terrible as people think him.
Soph. This old thiefe flatters, out of meere devotion,   10
To please the father for his second daughter.
Tra. But shall he have her?
Soph.   Yes, when I have Rome.
And yet the father's for him.
Mor.   Ile assure ye,
I hold him a good man.
Soph.   Yes sure a wealthy,
But whether a good womans man, is doubtfull.   15
Tra. Would 'twere no worse.
Mor.   What though his other wife,

Out of her most abundant stubbornes,
Out of her daily hue and cries upon him,
(For sure she was a Rebell) turn'd his temper,   *interpretation*
And forc'd him blow as high as she? do'st follow   *of Shrew* 20
He must retain that long since buried Tempest,
To this soft maid?   *pun ?*
    Soph.   I feare it.
    Tra.   So do I too:
And so far, that if God had made me woman,
And his wife that must be –
    Mor.   What would you doe sir?
    Tra. I would learn to eate Coales with an angry Cat,   25
And spit fire at him: I would (to prevent him)
Do all the ramping, roaring tricks, a whore
Being drunke, and tumbling ripe, would tremble at:
There is no safety else, nor morall wisdome,
To be a wife, and his.
    Soph.   So I should think too.   30
    Tra. For yet the bare remembrance of his first wife
(I tell ye on my knowledge, and a truth too)
Will make him start in's sleep, and very often
Cry out for Cudgels, Colstaves, any thing;
Hiding his Breeches, out of feare her Ghost   35
Should walk, and weare 'em yet. Since his first marriage,
He is no more the still *Petruchio*,
Then I am *Babylon.*
    Soph.   He's a good fellow,
And by my troth I love him: but to think
A fit match for this tender soule –   40
    Tra. His very frowne, if she but say her prayers
Louder then men talk treason, makes him tindar;   ♪♪
The motion of a Diall, when he's testy,
Is the same trouble to him as a water-worke;
She must do nothing of herselfe; not eate,   45

17   stubbornes,] MS; sobernesse, F1-2
39   And by my troth] MS; And on my word F1 *

Drink, say sir how do ye, make her ready, pisse,
Unlesse he bid her.
   Soph.   He will bury her,
Ten pound to twenty shillings, within these three weeks.
   Tra. Ile be your halfe.

Enter Jaques with a pot of Wine.

   Mor.   He loves her most extreamly,
And so long 'twil be honey-moon. Now *Jaques*   50
You are a busie man I am sure.
   Jaq.   Yes certaine,
This old sport must have egges,
   Soph. Not yet this ten daies.
   Jaq.   Sweet Gentlemen with Muskadell.
   Tra. That's right sir.
   Mor.   This fellow broods his Master: speed ye *Jaques.*
   Soph. We shall be for you presently.
   Jaq.   Your worships   55
Shal have it rich and neat: and o' my conscience
As welcom as our Lady day: O my old sir,
When shall we see your worship run at Ring?
That houre a standing were worth money.
   Mor.   So sir.
   Jaq. Upon my little honesty, your Mistris,   60
If I have any speculation, must thinke
This single thrumming of a Fiddle,
Without a Bow, but ev'n poore sport.
   Mor.   Y'are merry.
   Jaq. Would I were wise too: so God bless your worships.

Exit Jaq.

   Tra. The fellow tels you true.
   Soph.   When is the day man?   65
Come, come, you'l steale a marriage.
   Mor.   Nay, believe me:

46   pisse,] MS; unready F1 *
64   worships.] MS; worship. F1 *

But when her father pleases I am ready,
And all my friends shall know it.
   Tra.   Why not now?
One charge had serv'd for both.
   Mor.   There's reason in't.
   Soph. Call'd *Rowland.*
   Mor.   Will ye walke? They'l think we are lost: 70
Come Gentlemen.
   Tra.   You have wip't him now.
   Soph. So will he never the wench I hope.
   Tra.   I wish it.

Exeunt.

Scaena secunda.

Enter Rowland, and Livia.

   Row. Now Livia, if you'l goe away to night,
If your affections be not made of words –
   Liv. I love you, and you know how dearly *Rowland,*
Is there none neere us? my affections ever
Have been your servants; with what superstition   5
I have ever Sainted you –
   Row.   Why then take this way.
   Liv. Twill be a childish and a lesse prosperous course,
Then his that knows not care: why should we do
Our honest and our hearty love such wrong,
To over-run our fortunes?
   Row.   Then you flatter.   10
   Liv. Alas you know I cannot.
   Row.   What hope's left else
But flying to enjoy ye?
   Liv.   None so far,
For let it be admitted we have time,
And all things now in other expectation,

2   words——] Sympson; words. MS, F1 *

My father's bent against us; what but ruine,   15
Can such a by-way bring us? if your feares
Would let you look with my eyes, I would shew you,
And certain, how our staying here would win us
A course, though somewhat longer, yet far surer.
    Row. And then *Moroso* h'as ye.
    Liv.   No such matter: 20
For hold this certaine, begging, stealing, whoring,
Selling, (which is a sin unpardonable)
Of counterfeit Gods, or musty English Cracus,
Switches, or stones for th' toothache sooner finds me,
Then that drawn Fox *Moroso*.
    Row.   But his money,   25
If wealth may win you –
    Liv. If a Hog may be
High Priest among the Jewes: his money *Rowland*?
Oh Love forgive me, what a faith hast thou?
Why, can his money kisse me?
    Row.   Yes.
    Liv.   Behind,   30
Laid out upon a Petticote: or graspe me
While I cry, O good thank you? o' my troth
Thou makst me merry with thy feare: or lie with me,
As you may do? alas, what fooles you men are?
His mouldy money? half a dozen Riders,   35
That cannot sit but stampt fast to their Saddles?
No *Rowland*, no man shall make use of me;
My beauty was born free, and free Ile give it
To him that loves, not buys me. You yet doubt me.
    Row. I cannot say I doubt ye.
    Liv.   Goe thy waies,   40
Thou art the prettiest puling piece of passion:
Yfaith I will not faile thee.
    Row.   I had rather –

25 Fox] MS, F2 *; Fox and F1
29 what a faith] MS; what faith F1-2
31 Laid] MS, F2; Lasd F1

Liv. Prethee believe me, if I do not carry it,
For both our goods –
Row.   But –
Liv.   What but?
Row.   I would tell you.
Liv. I know all you can tell me; all's but this,   45
You would have me, and lie with me; is't not so?
Row. Yes.
Liv.   Why you shall; will that content you? *Goe.*
Row. I am very loth to goe.

Enter Byancha, and Maria.

Liv.   Now o' my conscience
Thou art an honest fellow: here's my sister;
Go, prethee goe; this kisse, and credit me,   50
Ere I am three nights older, I am for thee:
You shall heare what I do.
Row.   I had rather feel it.
Liv. Farewell.
Row.   Farewell.

Exit Rowland.

Liv.   Alas poore foole, how it looks?
It would ev'n hang it selfe, should I but crosse it.
For pure love to the matter I must hatch it.   55
Bya. Nay never look for merry houre *Maria*,
If now you make it not; let not your blushes,
Your modesty, and tendernesse of spirit,
Make you continuall Anvile to his anger:
Believe me, since his first wife set him going,   60
Nothing can bind his rage: Take your own Councell,
You shall not say that I perswaded you.
But if you suffer him –
Mar.   Stay, shall I do it?
Bya. Have you a stomack to't?
Mar.   I never shew'd it.

52-53   *Row.* I had rather feele it. / *Liv.* Farewell.] MS; *om.* F1 *

Bya. Twill shew the rarer, and the stranger in you.   65
But do not say I urg'd you.
    Mar.   I am perfect,
Like *Curtius* to redeeme my Countrey, have I
Leap'd into this gulph of marriage, and Ile do it.
Farewell all poorer thoughts, but spight & anger,
Till I have wrought a miracle. Now cosen,   70
I am no more the gentle tame *Maria*;
Mistake me not; I have a new soule in me
Made of a North-wind, nothing but tempest;
And like a tempest shall it make all ruins,
Till I have run my will out.
    Bya.   This is brave now,   75
If you continue it; but your own will lead you.
    Mar. Adieu all tendernesse, I dare continue;
Maides that are made of feares and modest blushes,
View me, and love example.
    Bya.   Here is your sister.
    Mar. Here is the brave old mans love.
    Bya.   That loves the young man. 80
    Mar. I and hold thee there wench: what a grief of heart is't,
When *Paphos* Revels should up rowse old night,
To sweat against a Cork; to lie and tell
The clock o'th lungs, to rise sport-starv'd?
    Liv.   Deere sister,
Where have you been you talke thus?
    Mar.   Why at Church, wench;   85
Where I am tide to talke thus: I am a wife now.
    Liv. It seems so, and a modest.
    Mar.   You are an asse;
When thou art married once, thy modesty
Will never buy thee Pins.
    Liv.   'Blesse me.
    Mar.   From what?
    Bya. From such a tame foole as our cozen *Livia*?   90

65   stranger] MS; stronger F1-2
82   Revels] MS, F2; Rebels F1

Liv. You are not mad.

Mar.   Yes wench, and so must you be,
Or none of our acquaintance, marke me *Livia.*
Or indeed fit for our sex: Tis bed time.
Pardon me yellow *Hymen,* that I meane
Thine offrings to protract, or to keepe fasting   95
My valiant Bridegroome.

Liv.   Whether will this woman?

Bya. You may perceive her end.

Liv.   Or rather feare it.

Mar. Dare you be partner in't?

Liv.   Leave it *Maria,*
I feare I have mark'd too much, for goodnesse leave it;
Devest you with obedient hands to bed.   100

Mar. To bed? No *Livia,* there are Comets hang
Prodigious over that yet; there's a fellow
Must yet before I know that heat (nere start wench)
Be made a man, for yet he is a monster;
Here must his head be *Livia.*

Liv.   Never hope it.   105
Tis as easie with a Sive to scoope the Ocean, as
To tame *Petruchio.*

Mar.   Stay: *Lucina* heare me,
Never unlock the treasure of my womb
For humane fruit, to make it capable;
Nor never with thy secret hand make briefe   110
A mothers labour to me; if I doe
Give way unto my married husbands will,
Or be a wife, in any thing but hopes,
Till I have made him easie as a child,
And tame as feare, he shall not win a smile,   115
Or a pleas'd look, from this austerity,
Though it would pull another Joynture from him,
And make him ev'ry day another man;
And when I kisse him, till I have my will,
May I be barren of delights, and know   120
Onely what pleasures are in dreams, and guesses.

Liv. A strange Exordium.

Bya.   All the severall wrongs
Done by Emperious husbands to their wives
These thousand yeeres and upwards, strengthen thee:
Thou hast a brave cause.

Mar.   And Ile doe it bravely   125
Or may I knit my life out ever after.

Liv. In what part of the world got she this spirit?
Yet pray *Maria*, looke before you truly,
Besides the disobedience of a wife,
Which you will finde a heavy imputation,   130
Which yet I cannot thinke your own, it shews
So distant from your sweetnesse.

Mar.   Tis I sweare.

Liv. Weigh but the person, and the hopes you have,
To worke this desperate cure.

Mar.   A weaker subject
Would shame the end I aime at, disobedience.   135
You talk too tamely: By the faith I have
In mine own Noble will, that childish woman
That lives a prisoner to her husbands pleasure,
Has lost her making, and becomes a beast,
Created for his use, not fellowship.   140

Liv. His first wife said as much.

Mar.   She was a foole,
And took a scurvy course; let her be nam'd
'Mongst those that wish for things, but dare not do 'em:
I have a new daunce for him, and a mad one.

Liv. Are you of this faith?

Bya.   Yes truly, and wil die in't.   145

Liv. Why then let's all weare breeches.

Bya.   That's a good wench,

Mar. Now thou comst neere the nature of a woman;
Hang these tame hearted Eyasses, that no sooner

---

129   disobedience] MS; obedience F1-2
144   him, and a mad one.] MS; him. F1 *
146   *Bya.* That's a good wench,] MS; *om.* F1 *

See the Lure out, and heare their husbands halla,
But cry like Kites upon 'em: The free Haggard   150
(Which is that woman, that hath wing, and knowes it,
Spirit, and plume) will make an hundred checks,
To shew her freedome, saile in ev'ry ayre,
And look out ev'ry pleasure; not regarding
Lure, nor quarry, till her pitch command   155
What she desires, making her foundred keeper
Be glad to fling out traines, and golden ones,
To take her down again.
    Liv.   You are learned sister;
Yet I say still, take heed.
    Mar.   A witty saying;
Ile tell thee *Livia*, had this fellow tired   160
As many wives as horses under him,
With spurring of their patience; had he got
A Patent, with an Office to reclaime us
Confirm'd by Parliament; had he all the malice
And subtilty of Devils, or of us,   165
Or any thing that's worse then both.
    Liv. Hey, hey boyes, this is excellent.
    Mar.   Or could he
Cast his wives new again, like Bels to make 'em
Sound to his will; or had the fearfull name
Of the first breaker of wilde women: yet,   170
Yet would I undertake this man, thus single,
And spight of all the freedom he has reach'd to,
Turn him and bend him as I list, and mold him
Into a babe again; that aged women,
Wanting both teeth & spleen, may Master him.   175
    Bya. Thou wilt be chronicl'd.
    Mar.   That's all I aime at.
    Liv. I must confesse, I do with all my heart
Hate an Emperious husband, and in time
Might be so wrought upon.
    Bya.   To make him cuckold?
    Mar. If he deserve it.

Liv.   Then Ile leave ye Ladies.   180

Bya. Thou hast not so much Noble anger in thee.

Mar. Goe sleep, goe sleep, what we intend to do,

Lies not for such starv'd soules as thou hast *Livia*.

     Liv. Good night: the Bridegroom will be with you presently.

     Mar. That's more then you know.

     Liv.   If ye worke upon him,   185

As you have promised, ye may give example,

Which no doubt will be followed.

     Mar. So.

     Bya.   Good night: we'l trouble you no further.

     Mar. If you intend no good, pray doe no harm.

     Liv. None, but pray for you.

Exit Livia.

By.   'Cheere wench.

Mar.   Now *Byancha*.   190

Those wits we have, let's wind 'em to the height,

My rest is up wench, and I pull for that

Will make me ever famous. They that lay

Foundations, are halfe builders all men say.

Enter Jaques.

     Jaq. My Master forsooth.   195

     Mar. Oh how do's thy Master? prethee commend me to him.

     Jaq. How's this? my Master staies forsooth.

     Mar. Why let him stay, who hinders him forsooth?

     Jaq. The Revel's ended now, to visit you.

     Mar. I am not sick.

     Jaq.   I mean to see his chamber, forsooth.   200

     Mar. Am I his Groom? where lay he last night, forsooth?

     Jaq. In the low matted Parlour.

     Mar. There lies his way by the long Gallery.

     Jaq. I mean your chamber: y'ar very merry Mistris.

     Mar. Tis a good signe I am sound hearted *Jaques*:   205

But if you'l know where I lie, follow me;

And what thou seest, deliver to thy Master.
   Bya. Do gentle *Jaques.*

Exeunt Maria and Byanca.

  Jaq.   Ha, is the wind in that dore?
By'r Lady we shall have foule weather then:
I doe not like the shuffling of these women,   210
They are mad beasts when they knock their heads together:
I have observ'd them all this day; their whispers,
One in anothers eare, their signes, and pinches,
And breaking often into violent laughters:
As if the end they purpos'd were their own.   215
Call you this weddings? Sure this is a knavery,
A very trick, and dainty knavery,
Marvellous finely carried, that's the comfort:
What would these women doe in waies of honour,
That are such Masters this way? Well, my Sir   220
Has been as good at finding out these toyes,
As any living; if he lose it now,
At his own perill be it. I must follow.

Exit.

Scena tertia.

*Enter Servants with lights, Petruchio, Petronius, Moroso, Tranio,
and Sophocles.*

  Petru. You that are married, Gentlemen, home at ye
For a round wager now.
    Soph.   Of this nights Stage?
    Petru.   Yes.
    Soph. I am your first man: a paire of Gloves of twenty shillings.
    Petru. Done: who takes me up next? I am for all bets.
    Mor. Faith lusty *Laurence*, were but my night now,   5
Old as I am, I would make you clap on Spurs,
But I would reach you, and bring you to your trot too:

5   Faith] MS; Well F1 *

I would Galants.

Petru. Well said good Will; but where's the stuffe boy, ha?
Old father time, your houre-glasse is empty.

Tra. A good tough traine would break thee all to pieces;   10
Thou hast not breath enough to say thy prayers.

Petron. See how these boyes despise us. Will you to bed sonne?
This pride will have a fall.

Petru.   Upon your daughter;
But I shall rise again, if there be truth
In Egges, and butter'd Pasnips.   15

Petro. Wil you to bed son, & leave talking;
Tomorrow morning we shall have you looke,
For all your great words, like St. *George* at Kingston,
Running a foot-back from the furious Dragon,
That with her angry tayle belabours him   20
For being lazie.

Soph.   His warlike launce
Bent like a crosse bow lath, alas the while.

Tra. His courage quench'd, and so far quench'd –
Petru. Tis well sir.

Tran.   That anie privie S^t even small St Davy
May lash him with a leeke.

Petru.   What then?   25

Soph. Fly, fly, quoth then the fearfull dwarfe;
Here is no place for living man.

Petru. Well my masters, if I doe sinke under my businesse
As I finde tis very possible, I am not the first
That has miscarried so; that's my comfort,   30
What may be done without impeach or waste,
I can and will doe.

Enter Jaques.

How now is my faire Bride a bed?

8   stuffe] MS; staffe F1 *
21-22 *Sopho.* His ... while.] MS; *om.* F1 *
24-25 *Tran.* That ... leek.] MS; *om.* F1 *
30   miscarried so;] Mason; miscarried so, MS; miscarried; So F1-2

Jaq.   No truly sir.

Petron. Not a bed yet? body o' me: we'l up
And rifle her: here's a coyle with a mayden-head,   35
Tis not intayl'd, is it?

Petru. If it be, ile try all the Law i'th land, but Ile cut it off:
Let's up, let's up, come.

Jaq.   That you cannot neither.

Petru.   Why?

Jaq. Unlesse you'll drop through the Chimney like a Daw,
Or force a breach i'th windows: you may untile the
House, tis possible.

Petru.   What dost thou meane?

Jaq. A morall sir, the Ballat will expresse it:
          The wind and the rain,
          Has turnd you back again,
          And you cannot be lodged there.   45
The truth is all the doores are baracadoed;
Not a Cathole, but holds a murd'rer in't.
She's victual'd for this moneth.

Petru.   Art not thou drunk?

Soph. He's drunk, he's drunk; come, come, let's up.

Jaq. Yes, yes, I am drunke: ye may goe up, ye may   50
Gentlemen, but take heed to your heads: I say no more.

Soph. Ile try that.

Exit Soph.

Petron.   How dost thou say? the door fast lock'd fellow?

Jaq. Yes truly sir, tis lock'd, and guarded too;
And two as desperate tongues planted behind it,
As ere yet batterd: they stand upon their honours,   55
And will not give up without strange composition,
Ile assure you; marching away with their Pieces cockt,
And Bullets in their mouthes will not satisfie them.

Petru. How's this? how's this they are?
Is there another with her?   60

Jaq. Yes marry is there, and an Engineir.

Mor. Who's that for Heavens sake?

Jaq.   Colonell Byancha, she commands the workes:
Spinola's but a ditcher to her, there's a halfe-moon:
I am but a poore man, but if you'l give me leave,   65
Ile venture a yeeres wages, draw all your force before it,
and mount your ablest piece of battery,
You shall not enter it these three nights yet.

Enter Sophocles.

Petru.   I should laugh at that good *Jaques.*
Soph.   Beat back again, she's fortified for ever.   70
Jaq.   Am I drunk now sir?
Soph.   He that dares most, goe up now, and be cool'd.
I have scap'd a pretty scowring.
Petru.   What are they mad? have we another Bedlam?
She doth not talke I hope?   75
Soph.   Oh terribly, extreamly fearfull,
The noise at London-bridge is nothing neere her.
Petru.   How got she tongue?
Soph.   As you got taile, she was born to't.
Petru.   Lock'd out a doors, and on my wedding-night?
Nay, and I suffer this, I may goe graze: 80
Come Gentlemen, Ile batter; are these vertues?
Soph.   Do, and be beaten off with shame, as I was:
I went up, came to th' doore, knockd, no body answered;
Knock'd lowder, yet heard nothing: would have broke in by force;
When suddenly a water-worke flew from the window   85
With such violence, that had I not duck'd
Quickly like a Fryer, *caetera quis nescit?*
The chamber's nothing but a meere Ostend,
In every window Pewter cannons mounted,
You'l quickly finde with what they are charg'd sir.   90
Petru.   Why then tantara for us.
Soph.   And all the lower works lin'd sure with small shot,
Long tongues with Fire-locks, that at twelve score blanke
Hit to the heart: now and ye dare go up.

75   She doth not] MS; They doe not F1 *

Enter Maria and Byanca above.

Mor. The window opens, beat a parley first;   95
I am so much amaz'd my very haire stands.
   Petron. Why, how now daughter: what intrenc'd?
   Mar. A little guarded for my safety sir.
   Petru. For your safety Sweet-heart? why who offends you?
I come not to use violence.   100
   Mar. I thinke you cannot sir, I am better fortified.
   Petru. I know your end, you would faine reprieve
Your Maiden-head a night, or two.
   Mar.   Yes,
Or ten, or twenty, or say an hundred;
Or indeed, till I list lie with you.   105
   Soph. That's a shrewd saying; from this present houre,
I never will believe a silent woman.
When they break out they are bonfires.
   Petro. Till you list lie with him? why who are you Madam?
   Bya. That trim Gentlemans wife, sir.   110
   Petru. Cry you mercy, do you command too?
   Mar. Yes marry do's she, and in chiefe.
   Bya. I doe command, and you shall go without:
(I mean your wife, for this night)
   Mar. And for the next too wench, and so as't follows. 115
   Petro. Thou wilt not, wilt 'a?
   Mar. Yes indeed deere father,
And till he seale to what I shall set down,
For anything I know, forever.
   Soph. Birlady these are Bugs-words.   120
   Tra. You heare sir, she can talke, God be thanked.
   Petru. I would I heard it not sir.
   Soph. I finde that all the pity bestowd upon this woman,
Makes but an Anagram of an ill wife,
For she was never vertuous.   125
   Petru. Youl let me in I hope, for all this jesting.
   Mar. Hope still Sir.

120   Birlady] MS; Indeed F1 *

Petron.   You will come down I am sure.

Mar. I am sure I will not.

Petron.   Ile fetch you then.

Bya. The power of the whole County cannot sir,

Unless we please to yeild, which yet I thinke   150

We shal not; charge when you please, you shall

Heare quickly from us.

Mor.   Heaven blesse me from

A Chicken of thy hatching, is this wiving?

Petru. Prethee *Maria* tell me what's the reason,

And do it freely, you deale thus strangely with me?   135

You were not forc'd to marry, your consent

Went equally with mine, if not before it:

I hope you do not doubt I want that mettle

A man should have to keepe a woman waking;

I would be sorry to be such a Saint yet: 140

My person, as it is not excellent,

So tis not old, nor lame, nor weak with Physick,

But wel enough to please an honest woman,

That keeps her house, and loves her husband.

Mar. Tis so.

Petru.   My means and my conditions are no shamers 145

Of him that owes 'em, all the world knows that,

And my friends no reliers on my fortunes.

Mar. All this I believe, and none of all these parcels

I dare except against; nay more, so far

I am from making these the ends I aime at,   150

These idle outward things, these womens feares,

That were I yet unmarried, free to choose

Through all the Tribes of man, i'ld take *Petruchio*

In's shirt, with one ten Groats to pay the Priest,

Before the best man living, or the ablest   155

That ev'r leap'd out of Lancashire, and they are right ones.

Petron. Why do you play the foole then, and stand prating

Out of the window like a broken Miller!

Petru. If you wil have me credit you *Maria*,

132   Heaven blesse] MS; 'Blesse F1; Bless F2

Come down, and let your love confirme it.   160
   Mar. Stay there sir, that bargain's yet to make.
   Bya. Play sure wench, the packs in thine own hand.
   Soph. Let me die lowsie, if these two wenches
Be not brewing knavery to stock a Kingdome.
   Petru. Death, this is a Riddle: 165
I love you, and I love you not.
   Mar.   It is so:
And till your own experience do untie it,
This distance I must keep.
   Petru.   If you talk more,
I am angry, very angry.
   Mar. I am glad on't, and I wil talke.   170
   Petru.   Prethee peace,
Let me not think thou art mad. I tell thee woman,
If thou goest forward, I am still *Petruchio.*
   Mar. And I am worse, a woman that can feare
Neither *Petruchio Furius*, nor his fame,
Nor any thing that tends to our allegeance;   175
There's a short method for you, now you know me.
   Petru. If you can carry't so, tis very wel.
   Bya. No you shall carry it, sir.
   Petru.   Peace gentle Low-bel.
   Petron. Use no more words, but come down instantly,
I charge thee by the duty of a child.   180
   Petru. Prethee come *Maria*, I forgive all.
   Mar. Stay there; That duty, that you charge me by
(If you consider truly what you say)
Is now another mans, you gave't away
I'th Church, if you remember, to my husband: 185
So all you can exact now, is no more
But onely a due reverence to your person,
Which thus I pay: Your blessing, and I am gone
To bed for this night.
   Petron.   This is monstrous:
That blessing that St *Dunstan* gave the Devil,   190

165   Death,] MS; Why F1 *

If I were neere thee, I would give thee –
Pull thee down by th' nose.

Bya.   Saints should not rave, sir;
A little Rubarb now were excellent.

Petru. Then by that duty you owe to me *Maria*,
Open the doore, and be obedient: I am quiet yet.   195

Mar. I do confesse that duty; make your best on't.

Petru. Why give me leave, I will.

Bya.   Sir, there's no learning
An old stiffe Jade to trot: you know the morall.

Mar. Yet as I take it sir, I owe no more
Then you owe back again.

Petru.   You wil not Article?   200
All I owe, presently, let me but up, ile pay.

Mar. Y'are too hot, and such prove Jades at length;
You do confesse a duty or respect to me from you again:
That's very neere, or full the same with mine?

Petru.   Yes.

Mar. Then by that duty, or respect, or what   205
You please to have it, goe to bed and leave me,
And trouble me no longer with your fooling;
For know, I am not for you.

Petru.   Well, what remedy?

Petron. A fine smart Cudgell. Oh that I were neer thee.

Bya. If you had teeth now, what a case were we in?   210

Mor. These are the most authentique Rebels, next
Tyrone, I ever read of.

Mar. A weeke hence, or a fortnight, as you beare you,
And as I finde my will observ'd, I may
With intercession of some friends be brought   215
Maybe to kisse you, and so quarterly
To pay a little rent by composition,
You understand me?

Soph.   Thou Boy, thou.

Petru. Well there are more Maides then *Maudlin*,
That's my comfort.

Mar.   Yes, and more men than *Michael*.   220

Petru.   I must not to bed with this stomach, and no meat Lady.

Mar.   Feed where you will, so it be sound, and wholsome,

Else live at livery, for i'le none with you.

By.   You had best back one of the dairy maids, they'l carry.

But take heed to your girthes, you'l get a bruise else.   225

Petru.   Now if thou would'st come down, and tender me:

All the delights due to a marriage bed,

Studdy such kisses as would melt a man,

And turne thy selfe into a thousand figures,

To adde new flames unto me, I would stand   230

Thus heavy, thus regardlesse, thus despising

Thee, and thy best allurings: all the beauty

That's laid upon your bodies, mark me well,

For without doubt your mind's are miserable,

You have no maskes for them: all this rare beauty,   235

Lay but the Painter, and the silke worme by,

The Doctor with his dyets, and the Taylor,

And you appeare like flead Cats, not so handsome.

Mar.   And we appeare like her that sent us hither,

That onely excellent and beauteous nature;   240

Truly ourselves, for men to wonder at,

But too divine to handle; we are Gold,

In our own natures pure; but when we suffer

The husbands stamp upon us, then alayes,

And base ones of you men are mingled with us,   245

And make us blush like Copper.

Petru.   Then, and never

Till then are women to be spoken of,

For till that time you have no soules I take it:

Good night: come Gentlemen; i'le fast for this night,

But by this hand – well: I shall come up yet?

Mar.   Noe.   250

Petru.   There will I watch thee like a wither'd Jewry,

Thou shalt neither have meat, fire, nor Candle,

Nor any thing that's easie: doe you rebell so soone?

Yet take mercy.

Bya.   Put up your Pipes: to bed sir; i'le assure you

A moneths seige will not shake us.

    Mor.   Well said Colonell.   255

    Mar. To bed, to bed *Petruchio*: good night Gentlemen,
You'l make my Father sicke with sitting up:
Here you shall finde us any time these ten dayes,
Unlesse we may march off with our contentment.

    Petru. Ile hang first.

    Mar.   And i'le quarter if I doe not,   260
Ile make you know, and feare a wife *Petruchio*,
There my cause lies.
You have been famous for a woman tamer,
and beare the fear'd-name of a brave wife-breaker:
A woman now shall take those honours off,   265
And tame you; nay, never look so bigge, she shall, beleeve me,
And I am she: what thinke ye; good night to all,
Ye shall finde Centinels.

    Bya.   If ye dare sally.

Exeunt above.

    Petro. The devill's in 'em, ev'n the very devill,
The downe right devill.   270

    Petru. Ile devill 'em: by these ten bones I will:
I'le bring it to the old Proverb, no sport no pie:
Death taken down i'th top of all my speed;
This is fine Dancing: Gentlemen, stick to me.
You see our Freehold's touch'd, and by this light,   275
We will beleaguer 'em, and either starve 'em out,
Or make 'em recreant.

    Petro. Ile see all passages stopt, but those about 'em:
If the good women of the Towne dare succour 'em,
We shall have warres indeed.

    Soph.   Ile stand perdue upon 'em.   280

    Mor. My regiment shall lye before.

    Jaq. I think so, 'tis grown too old to stand.

    Petru. Let's in, and each provide his tackle,

266   shall,] 1711 * ~_MS, F1-2
273   Death taken] MS; ——taken F1-2

We'l fire 'em out, or make 'em take their pardons,
Heare what I say, on their bare knees, I vow   285
Am I *Petruchio*, fear'd, and spoken of,
And on my wedding night am I thus jaded?

Exe. Omnes.

Scaena quarta.

Enter Rowland, and Pedro, at severall doores.

Row. Now *Pedro*?
Ped.   Very busie Master *Rowland*.
Row. What haste man?
Ped.   I beseech you pardon me,
I am not mine own man.
Row.   Thou art not mad?
Ped. No; but beleeve me, as hasty –
Row.   The cause good *Pedro*?
Ped. There be a thousand sir; you are not married?   5
Row. Not yet.
Ped.   Keepe your selfe quiet then.
Row.   Why?
Ped. You'l finde a Fiddle that never will be tun'd else:
From all such women deliver me.

Exit.
Enter Iaques.

Row. What ailes the fellow tro? *Iaques*?
Iaq.   Your friend sir.
But very full of businesse.
Row.   Nothing but businesse?   10
Prethee the reason; is there any dying?
Jaq. I would there were sir.
Row.   But thy businesse?

285 knees, I vow] MS; knees—— F1 *
8   all such women deliver me.] MS; all women—— F1 *

Iaq.   Ile tell you in a word, I am sent to lay
An imposition upon Sowse and Puddings,
Pasties, and Penny Custards, that the women   15
May not releeve yon Rebels: Fare ye well sir.
   Row.   How does my Mistresse?
   Iaq.   Like a resty jade.
She's spoil'd for riding.

                    Exit Iaques.

   Row.   What a devill ayle they?

                    Enter Sophocles.

Custards, and penney Pasties, Fooles and Fiddles,
What's this to'th purpose? O well met.
   Soph.   Now *Rowland.*   20
I cannot stay to talk long.
   Row.   What's the matter?
Here's stirring, but to what end? whether goe you?
   Soph.   To view the works.
   Row.   What workes?
   Soph.   The womens Trenches.
   Row.   Trenches? are such to see?
   Soph.   I doe not jest sir.
   Row.   I cannot understand you.
   Soph.   Doe not you heare   25
In what a state of quarrell the new Bride
Stands with her husband?
   Row.   Let him stand with her, and there's an end.
   Soph.   It should be, but by'r Lady
She holds him out at Pikes end, and defies him,   30
And now is fortifide; such a Regiment of Rutters
Never defied men braver: I am sent
To view their preparation.
   Row.   This is newes
Stranger then armies in the ayre, you saw not
My gentle Mistresse?
   Soph.   Yes, and meditating   35

34   armies] MS; Armes F1; Arms F2

Upon some secret businesse, when she had found it
She leapt for joy, and laugh'd, and straight retir'd
To shun *Moroso*.
 Row.   This may be for me.
 Soph. Will you along?
 Row.   No.
 Soph.   Farewell.

      Exit Sophocles.

 Row.   Farewell sir.
What should her musing meane, and what her joy in't, 40
If not for my advantage? Stay ye; may not

 Enter Livia at one doore, and Moroso at another harkning.

That Bob-taile Jade *Moroso*, with his Gold,
His gew-gaudes, and the hope she has to send him
Quickly to dust, excite this? here she comes,
And yonder walkes the Stallion to discover: 45
Yet i'le salute her: save you beauteous mistresse.
 Livi. The Fox is kennell'd for me: save you sir.
 Row. Why doe you look so strange?
 Liv.   I use to looke sir
Without examination.
 Mor. Twenty Spur-Royals for that word.
 Row.   Belike then 50
The object discontents you?
 Liv.   Yes it does.
 Row. Is't come to this? you know me, doe you not?
 Liv. Yes as I may know many by repentance.
 Row. Why doe you breake your faith?
 Liv.   Ile tell you that too,
You are under age, and no band holds upon you. 55
 Mor. Excellent wench.
 Liv.   Sue out your understanding,
And get more haire, to cover your bare knockle
(For Boyes were made for nothing, but dry kisses,)

57 knockle] MS; knuckle F1-2

And if you can, more manners.

Mor.   Better still.

Liv. And then if I want Spanish gloves, or stockings,   60
A ten-pound waste-coate, or a Nag to hunt on,
It may be I shall grace you to accept 'em.

Row. Farewell, and when I credit women more,
May I to Smith-field, and there buy a Jade,
(And know him to be so) that breakes my neck.   65

Liv. Because I have knowne you, Ile be thus kinde to you;
Farewell, and be a man, and i'le provide you,
Because I see y'are desperate, some staid Chamber-maid
That may relieve your youth, with wholesome doctrin.

Mor. She's mine from all the world: ha wench?

Liv.   Ha Chicken? – – – 70

gives him a box o'th eare and Ex.

Mor. How's this? I do not love these favours: save you.

Row. The devill take thee – – – –

wrings him byth' nose.

Mor.   Oh!

Row.   There's a love token for you:
                                   [thank me now.

Exit.

Mor. Ile thinke on some of ye, and if I live,
My nose alone shall not be plaid withall.   75

Exit.

73   S.D. *Exit.*] MS; *om.* F1-2

ACTUS SECUNDUS - - - - - - - - - - - - - - - - - *Scaena* **prima**

Enter Petronius, and Moroso.

Petro. A Box o'th eare doe you say?
Mor.   Yes sure a sound one,
Beside my nose blown to my hand; if *Cupid*
Shoot Arrows of that weight, i'le sweare devoutly,
Has sude his liverie, and no more a Boy.
    Petro. You gave her some ill language?
Mor.   Not a word,   5
    Petro. Or might be you weare fumbling?
Mor.   Would I had sir.
I had been a forehand then; but to be baffel'd,
And have no feeling of the cause –
    Petro.   Be patient,
I have a medicine clapt to her back will cure her.
    Mor. No sure it must be afore sir.
    Petro.   O' my Conscience,   10
When I got these two wenches (who till now
Ne'r shew'd their riding) I was drunck with Bastard,
Whose nature is to forme things like it selfe
Heady, and monstrous: did she slight him too?
    Mor. That's all my comfort: a meere Hobby-horse   15
She made childe *Rowland*: s'foot she would not know him,
Not give him a free look, not reckon him
Among her thoughts, which I held more then wonder,
I having seene her within's three dayes kisse him
With such an appetite as though she would eat him.   20

Petro.   There is some trick in this: how did he take it?

Mor.   Ready to cry; he ran away.

Petro.   I feare her.
And yet I tell you, ever to my anger,
She is as tame as Innocency; it may be
This blow was but a favour.

Mor.   Ile be sworne   25
'Twas well tye'd on then.

Petro.   Goe too, pray forget it,
I have bespoke a Priest: and within's two houres
Ile have ye married; will that please you?

Mor.   Yes.

Petro.   Ile see it done my selfe, and give the Lady
Such a sound exhortation for this knavery   30
Ile warrant you, shall make her smell this Moneth on't,

Mor.   Nay good sir, be not violent.

Petro.   Neither – – –

Mor.   It may be
Out of her earnest love, there grew a longing
(As you know women have such toyes) in kindnesse,
To give me a box o'the eare or so.

Petro.   It may be.   35

Mor.   I reckon for the best still: this night then
I shall enjoy her.

Petro.   You shall hansell her.

Mor.   Old as I am, i'le give her one blow for't
Shall make her groane this twelve-moneth.

Petro.   Where's your joynture?

Mor.   I have a joynture for her.

Petro.   Have your Councell   40
Perus'd it yet?

Mor.   No Councell, but the night, and your sweet daughter
Shall ere peruse that Joynture.

Petro.   Very well sir.

Mor.   Ile no demurrers on't nor no rejoynders.
The other's ready seal'd.

Petro.   Come then lets' comfort

My Son *Petruchio*, he's like little Children 45
That loose their Bables, crying ripe.
   Mor.   Pray tell me,
Is this stern woman still upon the flaunt
Of bold defiance?
   Petro.   Still, and still she shall be
Till she be starv'd out: you shall see such justice,
That women shall be glad after this tempest 50
To tye their husbands shooes, and walke their horses.
   Mor. That were a merry world: doe you heare the rumour,
They say the women are in Insurrection,
And meane to make a – – –
   Petro.   They'l sooner
Draw upon walls as we doe: Let 'em, let 'em, 55
We'l ship 'em out in Cuck stooles, there they'l saile
As brave *Columbus* did, till they discover
The happy Islands of obedience.
We stay too long, Come.
   Mor.   Now Saint *George* be with us.

Exeunt.

Scaena Secunda.

Enter Livia alone.

   Liv. Now if I can but get in hansomely,
Father I shall deceive you, and this night
For all your private plotting, i'le no wedlock;
I have shifted saile, and finde my Sisters safety
A sure retirement; pray to heaven that *Rowland* 5
Do not beleeve too farre, what I said to him,
For y'on old Foxcase forc'd me, that's my feare,
Stay, let me see, this quarter fierce *Petruchio*
Keepes with his Myrmidons: I must be suddaine,
If he seize on me, I can looke for nothing 10

52 *Mor.*] F2; *om.* F1

But Marshall Law; to this place have I scap'd him;
Above there.

Enter Maria and Byancha above.

Mar.   *Qui va la?*
Liv.   A Friend.
Bya.   Who are you?
Liv. Looke out and know.
Mar.   Alas poore wench, who sent thee,
What weake foole made thy tongue his Orator?
I know you come to parly.
    Liv.   Y'are deceiv'd,   15
Urg'd by the goodnes of your cause I come
To doe as you doe.
    Mar.   Y'ar too weake, too foolish,
To cheat us with your smoothnesse: doe not we know
Thou hast been kept up tame?
    Liv. Beleeve me.
    Mar.   No, prethee good *Livia*   20
Utter thy Eloquence somewhere else.
    Bya.   Good Cosen
Put up your Pipes; we are not for your palat,
Alas we know who sent you.
    Liv.   O' my faith.
    Bya. Stay there; you must not thinke your faith, or troth,
Or by your Maydenhead, or such Sonday oathes   25
Sworne after Even-Song, can inveigle us
To loose our hand-fast: did their wisdomes thinke
That sent you hither, we would be so foolish,
To entertaine our gentle Sister *Sinon*,
And give her credit, while the Woodden Jade   30
Petruchio stole upon us: no good Sister,
Goe home, and tell the merry Greekes that sent you,
Ilium shall burn, and I, as did *Æneas*,

12   *Qui va la?*] MS; Cheval'a. F1-2
23   O' my faith.] A my faith. MS; O' my word—— F1 *
24   faith, or troth,] MS; word, F1 *

will on my back, spite of the Myrmidons,
Carry this warlike Lady, and through Seas   35
Unknown, and unbeleev'd, seek out a Land,
Where like a race of noble *Amazons*,
We'le root our selves and to our endlesse glory
Live, and despise base men.
    Liv.   Ile second ye.
    Bya. How long have you been thus?
    Liv.   That's all one Cosen.   40
I stand for freedome now.
    Bya.   Take heed of lying;
For by this light, if we doe credit you,
And finde you tripping, his infliction
That kill'd the Prince of *Orenge*, will be sport
To what we purpose.
    Liv.   Let me feele the heaviest.   45
    Mar. Swear by thy Sweet-heart *Rowland* (for by your
                          [mayden-head,
I fear 'twill be too late to swear) you meane
Nothing but faire and safe, and honourable
To us, and to your selfe.
    Liv.   I sweare.
    Bya.   Stay yet,
Sweare as you hate *Moroso*, that's the surest,   50
And as you have a Christian feare to finde him
Worse then a poore dride Jack, full of more Aches
Then Autumne has; more knavery, and usury,
And foolery, and brokery, then doggs-ditch:
As you doe constantly beeleeve he's nothing   55
But an old empty bagge with a grey beard,
And that beard such a Bob-taile, that it lookes
Worse then a Mares taile eaten off with Fillyes:
As you acknowledge, that young hansome wench
That lyes by such a Bilbo blade, that bends   60
With ev'ry passe he makes to'th hilts, most miserable,
A dry nurse to his Coughes, a fewterer

51   Christian] MS; certaine F1 *

To such a nasty fellow, a rob'd thing
Of all delights youth lookes for: and to end,
One cast away on course beef, born to brush   65
That everlasting Cassock that has worne
As many Servants out, as the Northeast passage
Has consum'd Saylors: if you sweare this, and truly
Without the reservation of a gowne
Or any meritorious Petticoate,   70
'Tis like we shall beleeve you.
    Liv.   I doe sweare it.
    Mar. Stay yet a little; came this wholesome motion
(Deale truly Sister) from your own opinion,
Or some suggestion of the Foe?
    Liv.   Nev'r feare me,
For by that little faith I have in husbands,   75
And the great zeale I beare your cause, I come
Full of that liberty, you stand for, Sister.
    Mar. If we beleeve, and you prove recreant *Livia*,
Think what a maym you give the noble Cause
We now stand up for: Thinke what women shall   80
An hundred yeare hence speak thee, when examples
Are look'd for, and so great ones, whose relations
Spoke as we do 'em wench, shall make new customs.
    Bya. If you be false, repent, goe home, and pray,
And to the serious women of the City   85
Confesse your selfe; bring not a sinne so heynous
To load thy soule, to this place: mark me *Livia*,
If thou bee'st double, and betray'st our honours,
And we fail in our purpose: get thee where
There is no women living, nor no hope   90
There ever shall be.
    Mar.   If a Mothers daughter,
That ever heard the name of stubborn husband
Find thee, and know thy sinne.
    Bya.   Nay, if old age,
One that has worne away the name of woman,

93   Find] MS, F2; Found F1 *

And no more left to know her by, but railing,   95
No teeth, nor eyes nor legges, but woodden ones
Come but i'th wind-ward of thee, for sure she'l smell thee
Thou'lt be so ranck, she'l ride thee like a night-mare,
And say her Prayers back-ward to undoe thee,
She'l curse thy meat and drink, and when thou marriest,   100
Clap a sound spell for ever on thy pleasures.
 Mar. Children of five yeare old, like little Fayries
Will pinch thee into motley, all that ever
Shall live, and heare of thee, I meane all women;
Will (like so many furies) shake their Keyes,   105
And tosse their flaming distaffes o're their heads,
Crying Revenge: take heed, 'tis hideous:
Oh 'tis a fearefull office, if thou had'st
(Though thou bee'st perfect now) when thou çam'st hither,
A false Imagination, get thee gone,   101
And as my learned Cozen said repent,
This place is sought by soundnesse.
 Liv.   So I seeke it,
Or let me be a most despis'd example.
 Mar. I doe beleeve thee, be thou worthy of it.
You come not empty?
 Liv.   No, Here's Cakes, and cold meat,   115
And tripe of proofe: behold here's wine, and beere,
Be suddaine, I shall be surpriz'd else.
 Mar. Meet at the low Parlor doore, there lyes a close way:
What fond obedience you have living in you,
Or duty to a man, before you enter,   120
Fling it away, 'twill but defile our Offrings.
 Bya. Be wary as you come,
 Liv.   I warrant ye.

     Exeunt.

Scaena Tertia.

Enter Rowland and Tranio at severall doores.

Tra. Now *Rowland*?

Row.   How doe you?

Tra.   How do'st thou man?
Thou look'st ill:

Row.   Yes, pray can you tell me *Tranio*,
Who knew the devill first?

Tra.   A woman.

Row. So, were they not well acquainted?

Tra.   May be so,
For they had certaine Dialogues together.   5

Row. He sold her fruit, I take it?

Tra.   Yes, and Cheese
That choak'd all mankinde after.

Row.   Canst thou tell me
Whether that woman ever had a faith
After she had eaten?

Tra.   That's a Schoole question

Row.   No
'Tis no question, for beleeve me *Tranio*,   10
That cold fruit after eating, bread naught in her

F1 *, *except* MS *and* Dyce, *insert the following as scene three:*
                    Scaena Tertia.
                    Enter three Maides.
          1 *Mai.* How goes your businesse Girles?
          2 Afoot, and faire.
          3 If fortune favour us: away to your strength
        The Country Forces are ariv'd, be gone.
        We are discover'd else.
          1 Arme, and be valiant.
          2 Think of our cause.
          3 Our Justice.
          1 'Tis sufficient.
                    Exeunt.
Designation *Scaena Tertia.*] Dyce; *om.* MS; *Scaena quarta,* F1 *
  4   *Row.* So, were] MS; *Row.* Thou hast heard I am sure of Esculapius.
      So were F1; So. Were F2 *
 11   eating,] Sympson; ~ MS, F1-2

But windy promises, and chollick vowes
That broke out both wayes; thou ha'st heard I am sure
Of *Esculapius*, a farre famed Surgeon,
One that could set together quarter'd Traytors,   15
And make 'em honest men.
    Tra.   How do'st thou *Rowland*?
    Row. Let him but take, (if he dare doe a cure
Shall get him fame indeed) a faithlesse woman,
There will be credit for him, that will speake him,
A broken woman *Tranio*, a base woman,   20
And if he can cure such a rack of honour
Let him come here, and practise.
    Tra.   Now for heavens sake
Why what ayl'st thou *Rowland*?
    Row.   I am ridden *Tranio*.
And Spur-gald to the life of patience
(Heaven keepe my wits together) by a thing   25
Our worst thoughts are too noble for, a woman.
    Tra. Your Mistresse has a little frown'd it may be?
    Row. She was my Mistresse.
    Tra.   Is she not?
    Row.   No *Tranio*.
She has done me such disgrace, so spitefully,
So like a woman bent to my undoing,   30
That henceforth a good horse shall be my Mistresse,
A good Sword, or a Booke: and if you see her,
Tell her I doe beseech you, even for loves sake. – –
    Tra. I will *Rowland*.
    Row.   She may sooner
Count the good I have thought her,   35
Our old love and our friend-ship,
Shed one true teare, meane one houre constantly,
Be old, and honest, married, and a maide,

13   wayes; thou] MS; wayes. / *Row.* Thou F1-2
22   heavens] MS; honours F1 *
33   even for loves sake.——] F2; euer for loues sake MS; even for love
     sake.—— F1

Then make me see her more, or more beleeve her:
And now I have met a Messenger, farewell sir.   40

Exit.

Tra. Alas poore *Rowland*, I will doe it for thee:
This is that dogge *Moroso*, but I hope
To see him cold i'th mouth first 'er he enjoy her:
Ile watch this young man, desperate thoughts may seize him,
And if my purse, or councell can, i'le ease him.   45

Exit.

Scaena quarta.

Enter Petruchio, Petronius, Moroso, and Sophocles.

Petru. For looke you Gentlemen, say that I grant her
Out of my free and liberall love, a pardon,
Which you and all men else know she deserves not,
(*Teneatis amici*) can all the world leave laughing?
Petro. I thinke not.
Petru.   No by – – – they cannot;   5
For pray consider, have you ever read,
Or heard of, or can any man imagine.
So stiffe a Tomb boy, or so set a malice,
And such a brazen resolution,
As this young Crab-tree? and then answer me,   10
And marke but this too friends, without a cause,
Not a foule word comes crosse her, not a feare,
She justly can take hold on, and doe you thinke
I must sleepe out my anger, and endure it,
Sow pillows to her ease, and lull her mischiefe?   15
Give me a Spindle first: no, no my Masters,
Were she as faire as *Nell* a *Greece*, and house-wife,
As good as the wise Saylors wife, and young still,
Never above fifteene; and these tricks to it,

Designation *Scaena quarta.*] Dyce; *om.* MS; *Scaena quinta.* F1 *

She should ride the wild Mare once a week, she should. 20
(Believe me friends she should) I would tabor her,
Till all the Legions that are crept into her,
Flew out with fire i'th tailes.
    Soph.   Methinks you erre now,
For to me seems, a little sufferance
Were a far surer cure.
    Petru.   Yes, I can suffer, 25
Where I see promises of peace and amendment.
    Mor.   Give her a few conditions.
    Petru.   Ile be hangd first.
    Petro.   Give her a crab-tree-cudgell.
    Petru.   So I will;
And after it a flock-bed for her bones.
And hard egges, till they brace her like a Drum, 30
She shall be pamperd with — — —
She shall not know a stoole in ten moneths Gentlemen.
    Soph.   This must not be.

Enter Jaques.

    Jaq.   Arme, arme, out with your weapons,
For all the women in the Kingdom's on ye;
They swarm like waspes, and nothing can destroy 'em, 35
But stopping of their hive, and smothering of 'em.

Enter Pedro.

    Ped.   Stand to your guard sir, all the devils extant
Are broke upon us, like a cloud of thunder;
There are more women, marching hitherward,
In rescue of my Mistris, then ere turn'd taile 40
At Sturbridge Faire; and I believe, as fiery.
    Jaq.   The forlorn-hope's led by a Tanners wife,
I know her by her hide; a desperate woman:
She flead her husband in her youth, and made
Raynes of his hide to ride the Parish, her plackett 45

45-48   her plackett ... breech;] MS; *om.* F1 *

Lookes like the straights of Gibralter, still wider
Downe to the gulphe, all sun-burnt Barbary
Lyes in her breech; take 'em all together,
They are a genealogy of Jennets, gotten
And born thus, by the boysterous breath of husbands;   50
They serve sure, and are swift to catch occasion,
(I meane their foes, or husbands) by the fore-locks,
And there they hang like favours; cry they can,
But more for Noble spight, then feare: and crying
Like the old Gyants that were foes to Heaven,   55
They heave ye stoole on stoole, and fling main Potlids
Like massie rocks, dart ladles, tossing Irons,
And tongs like Thunderbolts, till overlayd,
They fall beneath the waight; yet still aspiring
At those Emperious Codsheads, that would tame 'em.   60
There's nere a one of these, the worst and weakest,
(Choose where you will) but dare attempt the raysing
Against the soveraigne peace of Puritans,
A May-pole, and a Morris, maugre mainly
Their zeale, and Dudgeon-daggers: and yet more,   65
Dares plant a stand of battring Ale against 'em,
And drinke 'em out o'th Parish.
     Soph. Lo you fierce *Petruchio*, this comes of your impatience.
     Ped. There's one brought in the Beares against the Cannons
Of two church-wardens, made it good, and fought 'em   70
& in the churchyard after even song.
     Jaq. Another, to her everlasting fame, erected
Two Ale-houses of ease: the quarter sessions
Running against her roundly; in which businesse
Two of the disannullers lost their night-caps: 75
A third stood excommunicate by the cudgell.
The Cunstable, to her eternall glory,
Drunke hard, and was converted, and the victor.
     Ped. Then are they victualed with pies and puddings,
(The trappings of good stomacks) noble Ale   80

70   of two church-wardens,] MS; Of the town, F1 *
71   & in the churchyard after even song.] MS; *om.* F1 *

the true defendor, Sawsages, and smoak'd ones,
If need be, such as serve for Pikes; and Porke,
(Better the Jewes never hated:) here and there
A bottle of Metheglin, a stout Britaine
That will stand to 'em; what else they want, they war for.   85
   Petru. Come to councell,
   Soph. Now you must grant conditions or the Kingdom
Will have no other talke but this.
   Petro.   Away then,
And let's advise the best.
   Soph.   Why doe you tremble?
   Mor. Have I liv'd thus long to be knockt o'th head,   90
With halfe a washing beetle? pray be wise sir.
   Petru. Come, something Ile doe; but what it is I know not.
   Soph. To councel then, and let's avoyd their follies.
Guard all the doors, or we shal not have a cloke left.

Exeunt.

Scaena quinta.

Enter three mayds, at severall doors.

   1. How goes the businesse girles?
   2.   A foot, and faire.
   3. If fortune favour us: away to your strength,
The Country forces are ariv'd; be gon
We are discovered else.
   1.   Arme, and be valiant.
   2. Think of our cause.
   3.   Our justice.
   1.   Tis sufficient.   5

Exeunt.

Designation *Scaena quinta.*] Dyce; *om.* F1 *

Scaena Sexta.

Enter Petronius, Petruchio, Moroso, Sophocles, and Tranio.

Petro. I am indifferent, though I must confesse,
I had rather see her carted.
    Tra.   No more of that sir.
    Soph. Are ye resolv'd to give her fair conditions?
Twill be the safest way.
    Petru.   I am distracted,
Would I had run my head into a halter   5
When I first woo'd her: if I offer peace,
She'l urge her own conditions, that's the devil.
    Soph. Why say she do?
    Petru.   Say, I am made an Asse, then;
I know her aime: may I with reputation
(Answer me this) with safety of mine honour,   10
(After the mighty mannage of my first wife,
Which was indeed a fury to this Filly,
After my twelve strong labours to reclaime her,
Which would have made *Don Hercules* horn mad,
And hid him in his hide) suffer this *Sicely*,   15
Ere she have warm'd my sheets, ere grappel'd with me,
This Pinck, this painted Foyst, this Cockle-boat,
To hang her Fights out, and defie me friends,
A wel known man of war? if this be equal,
And I may suffer, say, and I have done?   20
    Petron. I do not think you may.
    Tra.   You'l make it worse sir.
    Soph. Pray heare me good *Petruchio*: but ev'n now,
You were contented to give all conditions,
To try how far she would carry: Tis a folly,
(And you wil find it so) to clap the curb on,   25
Er you be sure it proves a naturall wildnesse,
And not a forc'd. Give her conditions,
For on my life this tricke is put into her.

Designation *Scaena Sexta.*] Colman; Weber, Dyce; *om.* MS; *Scena tertia.*
F1-2

Petron. I should believe so too.

Soph.   And not her own.

Tra. You'l finde it so.

Soph.   Then if she flownder with you,   30
Clap spurs on, and in this you'l deale with temperance,
Avoyd the hurry of the world.

Tra.   And loose.

Musick above.

Mor. No honour on my life, sir.

Petru.   I wil do it.

Petron. It seems they are very merry.

Enter Jaques.

Petru.   Why God hold it.

Mor. Now *Jaques*?

Jaq.   They are i'th flaunt, sir.

Soph.   Yes we heare 'em. 35

Jaq. They have got a stick of Fiddles, and they firke it
In wondrous waies, the two grand Capitanos,
(They brought the Auxiliary Regiments)
Daunce with their coats tuckt up to their bare breeches,
And bid the Kingdom kisse 'em, that's the burden;   40
They have got Metheglin, and audacious Ale,
And talke like Tyrants.

Petron.   How knowest thou?

Jaq.   I peep't in
At a loose Lansket.

Tra.   Harke.

Petron.   A Song, pray silence.

SONG.

> *A Health for all this day*
> *To the woman that bears the sway*   45
> *And wears the breeches;*
> *Let it come, let it come.*

40   bid the Kingdom kiss] MS, F2 *; bid them kiss F1
44-57   *A Health ... pound.*] F2; *om.* MS, F1

Let this health be a Seal,
For the good of the Common-weal
  the woman shall wear the breeches.   50

Let's drink then and laugh it
And merrily merrily quaff it
And tipple, and tipple a round
  here's to thy fool,
  and to my fool.   55
  Come, to all fools
though it cost us wench, many a pound.

  Enter above Maria, Bianca, a Citty wife, a Country wife,
    and 3 women.

Mor. They look out.
Petru.   Good ev'n Ladies.
Mar. Good you good ev'n sir.
Petru.   How have you slept to night?
Mar. Exceeding well sir.
Petru.   Did you not wish me with you? 60
Mar. No, believe me, I never thought upon you.
Cun. Is that he?
Bya. Yes.
Cun.   Sir?
Soph.   She has drunk hard, mark her hood.
Cun. You are – – –
Soph. Learnedly drunk, Ile hang else: let her utter.
Cun. And I must tell you, *viva voce* friend, 65
A very foolish fellow.
Tra.   There's an Ale figure.
Petru. I thank you *Susan Brotes.*
Cit.   Forward sister.
Cun. You have espoused here a hearty woman,
A comely, and couragious.
Petru.   Wel I have so.
Cun. And to the comfort of distressed damsels, 70
Weomen out-worn in wedlock, and such vessels,
This woman has defied you.

Petru.   It should seem so.
Cun. And why?
Petru.   Yes, can you tell?
Cun.   For thirteen causes.
Petru. Pray by your patience Mistris.
Cit.   Forward sister.
Petru. Do you mean to treat of all these?
Cit.   Who shall let her?   75
   Petro. Doe you heare, Velvet-hood, we come not now
To heare your doctrine.
   Cunt.   For the first, I take it,
It doth divide it selfe into seven branches.
   Petru. Harke you good *Maria*,
Have you got a Catechiser here?
   Tra.   Good zeale.   80
   Soph. Good three pil'd predication, will you peace,
And heare the cause we come for?
   Cunt.   Yes Bob-tailes
We know the cause you come for, here's the cause,
But never hope to carry her, never dream
Or flatter your opinions with a thought   85
Of base repentance in her.
   Cit.   Give me sack,
By this, and next strong Ale.
   Cun.   Sweare forward sister.
   Cit. By all that's cordiall, in this place we'l bury
Our bones, fames, tongues, our triumphs; and then all
That ever yet was chronicl'd of woman;   90
But this brave wench, this excellent despiser,
This bane of dull obedience, shall inherit
Her liberall wil, and march off with conditions
Noble, and worth her selfe.
   Cun.   She shall *Tom Tilers*,
And brave ones too; My hood shal make a hearse-cloth,   95
And I lie under it, like *Jone o Gaunt*,
Ere I goe lesse, my Distaffe stucke up by me,

93   Her] MS; His F1-2

For the eternall Trophee of my conquests;
And loud fame at my head, with two main Bottles,
Shall fill to all the world the glorious fall   100
Of old *Don Gillian*.
    Cit.   Yet a little further,
We have taken Armes in rescue of this Lady;
Most just and Noble: if ye beat us off
Without conditions, and we recreant,
Use us as we deserve; and first degrade us   105
Of all our ancient chambring: next that
The Symbols of our secrecy, silke Stockings,
Hew of our heeles; our petticotes of Armes
Teare of our bodies, and our Bodkins breake
Over our coward heads.
    Cun.   And ever after   110
To make the tainture most notorious,
At all our Crests, *videlicet* our Plackets,
Let Laces hang, and we returne againe
Into our former titles, Dayry maids.
    Petru. No more wars: puissant Ladies, shew conditions,   115
And freely I accept 'em.
    Mar.   Call in *Livia*;
She's in the treaty too.

Enter Livia above.

    Mor.   How, *Livia*?
    Mar. Heare you that sir?
There's the conditions for ye, pray peruse 'em.
    Petron. Yes, there she is: t' had been no right rebellion, 120
Had she held off; what think you man?
    Mor.   Nay nothing.
I have enough o'th prospect: o'my conscience,
The worlds end, and the goodnesse of a woman
Will come together.
    Petron.   Are you there sweet Lady?

104   recreant,] MS; recant, F1-2
112   Plackets,] MS; Plackets. F1-2

Liv. Cry you mercy sir, I saw you not: your blessing.   125
Petron. Yes when I blesse a jade, that stumbles with me.
How are the Articles?
Liv.   This is for you sir;
And I shal think upon't.
Mor.   You have us'd me finely.
Liv. There's no other use of thee now extant,
But to be hung up; cassock, cap, and all,   130
For some strange monster at Apothecaries.
Petron. I heare you whore.
Liv.   It must be his then sir,
For need wil then compell me.
Cit.   Blessing on thee.
Liv. He wil undoe me in meere pans of Coles
To make him lustie.
Petron.   There's no talking to 'em;   135
How are they sir?
Petru.   As I expected:

Reads.

                         Liberty and clothes,
When, and in what way she wil: continuall moneys,
Company, and all the house at her dispose;
No tongue to say, why is this? or whether wil it;
New Coaches, and some buildings, she appoints here;   140
Hangings, and hunting-horses: and for Plate
And Jewels for her private use, I take it,
Two twousand pound in present: then for Musick,
And women to read French;
Petron.   This must not be.
Petru. And at the latter end a clause put in,   145
That *Livia* shal by no man be importun'd,
This whole moneth yet, to marry.
Petron.   This is monstrous.
Petru. This shall be done, Ile humor her awhile:
If nothing but repentance, and undoing
Can win her love, Ile make a shift for one.   150

Soph. When ye are once a bed, all these conditions
Lie under your own seale.
  Mar.   Do you like 'em?
  Petru.   Yes.
And by that faith I gave you fore the Priest
Ile ratifie 'em.
  Cun. Stay, what pledges?
  Mar. No, Ile take that oath;   155
But have a care you keep it.
  Cit.   Tis not now
As when *Andrea* liv'd.
  Cun.   If you do juggle,
Or alter but a Letter of these Articles
We have set down, the self-same persecution.
  Mar. Mistrust him not.
  Petru.   By all my honesty – – – 160
  Mar. Enough. I yield.
  Petron.   What's this inserted here?
  Soph. That the two valiant women that command here
Shall have a Supper made em, and a large one,
And liberall entertainment without grudging,
And pay for all their Souldiers.
  Petru.   That shall be too; 165
And if a tun of Wine wil serve to pay 'em,
They shall have justice: I ordaine ye all
Pay-masters, Gentlemen.
  Tra.   Then we shall have sport boyes.
  Mar. We'l meet you in the Parlour.
  Petru. Ne'r looke sad sir, for I will doe it. 170
  Soph. There's no danger in't.
  Petru. For *Livia's* Article, you shall observe it,
I have tyde my selfe.
  Petron.   I wil.
  Petru.   Along then: now
Either I break, or this stiffe plant must bow.

       Exeunt.

Enter Tranio, and Rowland.

Tra. Come, you shall take my counsell.
Row.   I shall hang first.
Ile no more love, that's certaine, tis a bane,
(Next that they poyson Rats with) the most mortall:
No, I thank Heaven I have got my sleep again,
And now begin to write sence; I can walk ye   5
A long howre in my chamber like a man,
And think of something that may better me;
Some serious point of Learning, or my state;
No more ay-mees, and misereri's, *Tranio*
Come neer my brain. Ile tell thee, had the devil   10
But any essence in him of a man,
And could be brought to love, and love a woman,
Twould make his head ake worser then his hornes doe;
And firke him with a fire he never felt yet,
Would make him dance. I tell thee there is nothing   15
(It may be thy case *Tranio*, therefore heare me:)
Under the Sun (reckon the masse of follies
Crept into th'world with man) so desperate,
So madde, so sencelesse, poor and base, so wretched,
Roguy, and scurvy.
Tra.   Whether wilt thou *Rowland*?   20
Row. As tis to be in love.
Tra.   And why for heavens sake?

9   misereri's,] Colman; Mistrisses, MS, F2; miseries F1

Row. And why for heavens sake? do'st thou not concieve me?
Tra. No by my troth.
Row.   Pray then, and hartely
For fear thou fall into't: I'le tell thee why too,
(For I have hope to save thee) when thou lovest,   25
And first beginst to worship the gilt calfe,
Imprimis, thou hast lost thy gentry,
And like a prentice flung away thy freedome.
Forthwith thou art a slave.
    Tra.   That's a new Doctrine.
    Row. Next thou art no more man.
    Tra.   What then?
    Row.   A Fryppery;   30
Nothing but brayded haire, and penny riband,
Glove, garter, ring, rose, or at best a swabber,
If thou canst love so neer to keep thy making,
Yet thou wilt loose thy language.
    Tra.   Why?
    Row.   O *Tranio,*
Those things in love, ne'r talke as we do,
    Tra.   No?   35
    Row. No without doubt, they sigh and shake the head,
And sometimes whistle dolefully.
    Tra.   No tongue?
    Row. Yes *Tranio,* but no truth in't, nor no reason,
And when they cant (for tis a kind of canting)
Ye shall hear, if you reach to understand 'em   40
(Which you must be a foole first, or you cannot)
Such gibbrish; such believe me, I protest Sweet,
And oh deer Heavens, in which such constellations
Raigne at the births of lovers, this is too well,
And daigne me Lady, daigne me I beseech ye   45
You poor unworthy lump, and then she licks him.
    Tra. A pox on't, this is nothing.

21   heavens] MS; vertue F1 *
22   heavens] MS; vertues F1 *
47   pox] MS; —— F1-2

Row.   Thou has'st hit it:
Then talks she ten times worse, and wryes and wriggles,
As though she had the itch (and so it may be).
   Tran. Of what religion are they,
Row.   Good old Catholikes,   50
They deale by intercession all, they keepe
A kind of household Gods, call'd chamber-maides,
Which being pray'd to, and their offerings brought,
(W.ch are in gold, yet some observe the old law
And guie 'em flesh) probatum est, you shall have   55
As good love for your monie, and as tydie
As ere you turn'd your legge ore, and that ended.
   Tra. Why thou art grown a strange discoverer.
   Row. Of mine own follies *Tranio.*
   Tra.   Wilt thou *Rowland,*
Certaine ne'r love again?
   Row.   I think so, certaine   60
And if I be not dead drunk, I shall keep it.
   Tra. Tell me but this; what do'st thou think of women?
   Row. Why as I think of fiddles, they delight me,
Till their strings break.
   Tra.   What strings?
   Row.   Their modesties,
Faithes, vowes and maidenheads, for they are like Kits   65
They have but foure strings to 'em.
   Tra.   What wilt thou
Give me for ten pound now, when thou next lovest,
And the same woman still?
   Row.   Give me the money;
A hundred, and my Bond for't.
   Tra.   But pray hear me,
I'le work all meanes I can to reconcile ye: 70
   Row. Do, do, give me the money.
   Tra.   There.
   Row.   Work *Tranio.*
   Tra. You shall go sometimes where she is.

50-57 *Tran.* Of what religion ... and that ended.] MS; *om.* F1 *

Row.   Yes straight.
This is the first good I ere got by woman.
    Tra. You would think it strange now, if an other beauty
As good as hers, say better.
    Row.   Well.
    Tra.   Conceive me,   75
This is no point o'th wager.
    Row.   That's all one.
    Tra. Love you as much, or more, then she now hates you.
    Row. Tis a good hearing, let 'em love: ten pound more,
I never love that woman.
    Tra.   There it is;
And so an hundred, if you lose.
    Row.   Tis done;   80
Have you an other to put in?
    Tra.   No, no sir.
    Row. I am very sorry: now will I erect
A new Game and go hate for th'bell; I am sure
I am in excellent case to win.
    Tra.   I must have leave
To tell you, and tell truth too, what she is,   85
And how shee suffers for you.
    Row.   Ten pound more,
I never believe you.
    Tra.   No sir, I am stinted.
    Row. Well, take your best way then.
    Tra.   Let's walk, I am glad
Your sullen feavor's off.
    Row.   Shal't see me *Tranio*
A monstrous merry man now: let's to the Wedding,   90
And as we go, tell me the generall hurry
Of these madde wenches, and their workes.
    Tra.   I will.
    Row. And do thy worst.
    Tra.   Something i'le do.
    Row.   Do *Tranio.*
                Exeunt.

Scaena Secunda.

Enter Pedro, and Jaques.

Ped. A paire of stocks bestride 'em, are they gone?

Jaq. Yes they are gon; and all the pans i'th Town
Beating before 'em: what strange admonitions
They gave my Master, and how fearfully
They threaten'd, if he brok 'em?

Ped.   O' my conscience   5
H'as found his full match now.

Jaq.   That I believe too.

Ped. How did she entertaine him?

Iaq.   She lookt on him.

Ped. But scurvely.

Iaq.   Faith with no great affection
That I saw: and I heard some say he kiss'd her,
But 'twas upon a treaty, and some coppies   10
Say but her cheek.

Ped.   Faith *Iaques,* what wouldst thou give
For such a wife now?

Iaq.   Full as many prayers
As the most zealous Puritane conceives
Out of the meditation of fat veale,
Or birds of prey, cram'd capons, against Players,   15
And to as good a tune too, but against her:
That heaven would blesse me from her: mark it *Pedro.*
If this house be not turn'd within this fortnight
With the foundation upward, i'le be carted.
My comfort is yet that those Amorities,   20
That came to back her cause, those heathen whores
Had their hoods hallowed with sack.

Ped.   How div'lish drunk they were?

Jaq. And how they tumbled, *Pedro,* didst thou marke
The Countrey Cavaliero?

---

8   Faith] MS; *om.* F1 *
11   Faith] MS; *om.* F1 *

Ped.   Out upon her,
How she turn'd down the Bragget?
Jaq.   I that sunke her.   25
Ped.   That drink was wel put to her; what a somer salt
When the chaire fel, she fetch'd, with her heels upward?
Jaq.   And what a piece of Landskip she discovered?
Ped.   Didst mark her, when her hood fel in the Posset?
Jaq.   Yes, and there rid, like a Dutch hoy; the Tumbrel,   30
When she had got her ballasse.
Ped.   That I saw too.
Jaq.   How faine she would have drawn on *Sophocles*
To come aboord, and how she simperd it – –
Ped.   I warrant her, she has been a worthy striker.
Iaq.   I'th heat of Summer there had been some hope on't.   35
for then old woeman are coole cellars.
Ped.   Hang her.
Jaq.   She offerd him a Harry-groat, and belcht out,
Her stomack being blown with Ale, such Courtship,
Upon my life has givn him twenty stooles since:
Believe my calculation, these old women   40
When they are tippled, and a little heated
Are like new wheels, theyl roare you all the Town o're
Till they be greasd.
Ped.   The City *Cinque-a-pace*
Dame Tost and Butter, had her Bob too?
Jaq.   Yes,
But she was sullen drunk, and given to filching,   45
I see her offer at a Spoon; my master – –
I do not like his looke, I feare h'as fasted
For all this preparation; lets steale by him.

Exeunt.

---

25   Bragget?] MS, F2; Bagget? F1
36   for then old woemen are coole cellars.] MS; *om.* F1 *
44   Tost] MS, F2; tosse F1
     her] MS; he F1; the F2
46   master—] F2; ~.MS, F1

Scena tertia.

Enter Petruchio, and Sophocles.

Soph. Not let you touch her all this night?
Petru.   Not touch her.
Soph. Where was your courage?
Petru.   Where was her obedience?
Never poore man was sham'd so; never Rascall
That keeps a stud of whores was us'd so basely.
    Soph. Pray you tell me one thing truly; do you love her?   5
    Petru. I would I did not, upon that condition
I past thee halfe my Land.
    Soph.   It may be then, -
Her modesty requir'd a little violence?
Some women love to struggle.
    Petru.   She had it,
And so much that I sweat for't, so I did,   10
But to no end: I washt an Ethiope;
She swore my force might weary her, but win her
I never could, nor should, till she consented;
And I might take her body prisoner,
But for her mind or appetite – – –
    Soph.   Tis strange;   15
This woman is the first I ever read of,
Refus'd a warranted occasion,
And standing on so faire termes.
    Petru.   I shall quit her.
    Soph. Us'd you no more art?
    Petru.   Yes, I swore to her,
And by no little ones, if presently   20
Without more disputation on the matter,
She grew not neerer to me, and dispatcht me
Out of the pain I was, for I was nettl'd,
And willingly, and eagerly, and sweetly,
I would to her Chamber-maid, and in her hearing   25
Begin her such a huntes-up.
    Soph.   Then she started?

Petru. No more then I do now; marry she answered
If I were so dispos'd, she could not help it;
But there was one cal'd *Iaques*, a poor Butler
One that might well content a single woman.   30
   Soph. And he should tilt her.
   Petru.   To that sence, and last
She bad me yet these six nights look for nothing,
Nor strive to purchase it, but faire good night,
And so good morrow, and a kisse or two
To close my stomach, for her vow had seald it,   35
And she would keep it constant.
   Soph.   Stay ye, stay ye,
Was she thus when you woo'd her?
   Petru.   Nothing *Sophocles*,
More keenely eager, I was oft afraid
She had bin light, and easy, she would showre
Her kisses so upon me.
   Soph.   Then I fear   40
An other spoke's i'th wheele.
   Petru.   Now thou hast found me,
There gnawes my deville, *Sophocles*, O patience
Preserve me; that I make her not example
By some unworthy way; as fleaing her,
Boyling, or making verjuce, drying her.   45
   Soph. I hear her.
   Petru.   Mark her then, and see the heire
Of spight and prodigality, she has studied
A way to begger's both, and by this hand

   Maria at the dore, and Servant and woman.

She shall be if I live a Doxy.
   Soph.   Fy Sir.
   Mar. I do not like that dressing, tis too poor,   50
Let me have six gold laces, broad and massy,
And betwixt ev'ry lace a rich embroydry,
Line the gown through with plush, perfum'd, and purffle
All the sleeves down with pearle.

Petru.   What think you *Sophocles.*
In what point stands my state now?
Mar.   For those hangings   55
Let 'em be carried where I gave appointment,
They are too base for my use, and bespeak
New pieces of the civill wars of France,
Let 'em be large and lively, and all silke work,
The borders gold.
    Soph.   I marry sir, this cuts it.   60
    Mar. That fourteen yardes of satten give my woman,
I do not like the colour, tis too civill:
Ther's too much silk i'th lace too; tell the Dutchman
That brought the mares, he must with all speed send me
An other suit of horses, and by all meanes   65
Ten cast of Hawkes for th' River, I much care not
What price they beare, so they be sound, and flying,
For the next winter, I am for the Country;
And mean to take my pleasure; wher's the horse man?
    Petru. She meanes to ride a great horse.
    Soph.   With a side sadle?   70
    Petru. Yes, and shee'l run a tilt within this twelve-month
    Mar. To morrow Ile begin to learne, but pray sir
Have a great care he be an easy doer,
Twill spoyle a Scholler els.
    Soph.   An easy doer,
Did you hear that?
    Petru.   Yes, I shall meet her morals   75
Er it be long I fear not.
    Mar.   O good morrow.
    Soph. Good morrow Lady, how is't now?
    Mar.   Faith sickly,
This house stands in an ill ayre.
    Petru.   Yet more charges?
    Mar. Subject to rots, and rheums; out on't, tis nothing
But a tild fog.
    Petru. What think you of the Lodge then?   80

80 think you of] MS, F2; think of F1

Mar. I like the seate, but tis too little, *Sophocles*
Let me have thy opinion, thou hast judgement.
　　Petru. Tis very well.
　　Mar.　　　　　　　What if I pluck it down,
And built a square upon it, with two courts
Still rising from the entrance?
　　Petru.　　　　　　　　And i'th midst　　　　　　85
A Colledge for young Scolds.
　　Mar.　　　　　　　And to the Southward
Take in a garden of some twenty acres,
And cast it off the Italian fashion, hanging.
　　Petru. And you could cast your self so too; pray Lady
Will not this cost much money?
　　Mar.　　　　　　　Some five thousand,　　　　90
Say six: Ile have it battel'd too.
　　Petru.　　　　　　　And gilt; *Maria,*
This is a fearfull course you take, pray think on't,
You are a woman now, a wife, and his
That must in honesty, and justice look for
Some due obedience from you.
　　Mar.　　　　　　　That bare word　　　　　95
Shall cost you many a pound more, build upon't;
Tell me of due obedience? what's a husband?
What are we married for, to carry sumpters?
Are we not one peece with you, and as worthy
Our own intentions, as you yours?
　　Petru.　　　　　　　Pray hear me.　　　　　100
　　Mar. Take two small drops of water, equall weigh'd,
Tell me which is the heaviest, and which ought
First to discend in duty?
　　Petru.　　　　　　You mistake me;
I urge not service from you, nor obedience
In way of duty, but of love, and credit;　　　　　105
All I expect is but a noble care
Of what I have brought you, and of what I am,
And what our name may be.
　　Mar.　　　　　　　That's in my making.

Petru. Tis true it is so.

Mar.   Yes it is *Petruchio*,
For there was never man without our molding,   110
Without our stampe upon him, and our justice,
Left any thing three ages after him
Good, and his own.

   Soph.   Good Lady understand him.

   Mar. I do too much, sweet *Sophocles*, he's one
Of a most spightfull self condition,   115
Never at peace with any thing but age,
That has no teeth left to return his anger:
A Bravery dwels in his blood yet, of abusing
His first good wife; he's sooner fire then powder,
And sooner mischief.

   Petru.   If I be so sodain   120
Do not you fear me?

   Mar.   No nor yet care for you,
And if it may be lawfull, I defie you:

   Petru. Do's this become you now?

   Mar.   It shall become me.

   Petru. Thou disobedient, weak, vain-glorious woman,
Were I but half so wilfull, as thou spightfull,   125
I should now drag thee to thy duty.

   Mar.   Drag me?

   Petru. But I am friends again: take all your pleasure.

   Mar. Now you perceive him *Sophocles*.

   Petru.   I love thee
Above thy vanity, thou faithlesse creature.

   Mar. Would I had been so happy when I married,   130
But to have met an honest man like thee,
For I am sure thou art good, I know thou art honest,
A hansome hurtlesse man, a loving man,
Though never a penny with him; and those eyes,
That face, and that true heart; weare this for my sake,   135
And when thou thinkst upon me pity me:
I am cast away,

                    Exit Mar.

Soph.   Why how now man?
Petru.   Pray leave me,
And follow your advices.
    Soph.   The man's jealous:
    Petru. I shall find a time ere it be long, to aske you
One or two foolish questions.
    Soph.   I shall answer   140
As wel as I am able, when you call me:
If she mean true, tis but a little killing,
And if I do not venture it, rots take me.
Farewel sir.

                    Exit Soph.

    Petru. Pray farewell. Is there no keeping
A wife to one mans use? no wintering   145
These cattell without straying? tis hard dealing,
Very hard dealing, Gentlemen, strange dealing:
Now in the name of madnesse, what star raign'd,
What dog-star, bull, or bear-star, when I married
This second wife, this whirwind, that takes all   150
Within her compasse? was I not wel warnd,
(I thought I had, and I believe I know it,)
And beaten to repentance in the daies
Of my first doting? had I not wife enough
To turn my tooles to? did I want vexation,   155
Or any speciall care to kill my heart?
Had I not ev'ry morning a rare breakfast,
Mixt with a learned Lecture of ill language,
Louder then *Tom* o'Lincoln; and at dinner,
A dyet of the same dish? was there evening   160
That ere past over us, without thou knave,
Or thou whore, for digestion? had I ever
A pull at this same poor sport men run mad for,
But like a cur I was faine to shew my teeth first,
And almost worry her? and did Heaven forgive me,   165

143   venture it, rots take me.] MS; venture its —— F1; venture it's F2
155   tooles] MS; love F1 *

And take this Serpent from me? and am I
Keeping tame devils now again? my heart akes;
Something I must do speedily: Ile die,
If I can hansomely, for that's the way
To make a Rascall of her; I am sick,   170
And Ile go very neer it, but Ile perish.

Exit.

Scaena Quarta.

Enter Livia, Byancha, Tranio, and Rowland.

Liv. Then I must be content sir, with my fortune.
Row. And I with mine.
Liv.   I did not think, a look,
Or a poore word or two, could have displanted
Such a fix'd constancy, and for your end too.
Row. Come, come, I know your courses: there's your gewgaws, 5
Your Rings, and Bracelets, and the Purse you gave me,
The money's spent in entertaining you
At Plays, and Cherry-gardens.
Liv.   There's your Chain too.
But if you'l give me leave, Ile weare the haire still;
I would yet remember you.
Bya.   Give him his love wench;   10
The young man has imployment for't.
Tra.   Fie *Rowland*.
Row. You cannot fie me out a hundred pound
With this poore plot: yet, let me nere see day more,
If something do not struggle strangely in me.
Bya. Young man, let me talk with you.
Row.   Wel young woman.   15
Bya. This was your Mistris once.
Row.   Yes.
Bya.   Are ye honest?

5   there's your] MS, F2; there's no F1

I see you are young, and hansome.

    Row.   I am honest.

    Bya. Why that's wel said: and there's no doubt your judgement
Is good enough, and strong enough to tell you
Who are your foes, and friends: why did you leave her?   20

    Row. She made a puppy of me.

    Bya.   Be that granted:
She must doe so sometimes, and oftentimes;
Love were too serious else.

    Row.   A witty woman.

    Bya. Had you lov'd me – – –

    Row.   I would I had.

    Bya.   And deerly;
And I had lov'd you so: you may love worse sir,   25
But that is not materiall.

    Row.   I shall loose.

    Bya. Some time or other for variety
I should have cal'd you foole, or boy, or bid you
Play with the Pages: but have lov'd you stil,
Out of all question, and extreamly too;   30
You are a man made to be loved:

    Row.   This woman
Either abuses me, or loves me dearely.

    Bya. Ile tell you one thing, if I were to choose
A husband to mine own mind, I should think
One of your mothers making would content me,   35
For o'my conscience she makes good ones.

    Row.   Lady,
Ile leave you to your commendations:
I am in again, The divel take their tongues.

    Bya. You shall not goe.

    Row.   I will: yet thus far *Livia*,
Your sorrow may induce me to forgive you,   40
But never love again; if I stay longer,
I have lost two hundred pound.

    Liv.   Good sir, but thus much – –

32   dearely.] MS; deadly. F1 *

Tra. Turn if thou beest a man.

Liv.   But one kisse of you;
One parting kisse, and I am gone too.

Row.   Come,
I shall kisse fifty pound away at this clap: 45
We'l have one more, and then farewel.

Liv.   Farewel.

Bya. Wel, go thy waies, thou bearst a kind heart with thee.

Tra. H'as made a stand.

Bya.   A noble, brave young fellow,
Worthy a wench indeed.

Row.   I wil: I wil not.

Exit Rowland.

Tra. He's gone: but shot agen; play you but your part,   50
And I will keep my promise: forty Angels
In fair gold Lady: wipe your eyes: he's yours
If I have any wit.

Liv.   Ile pay the forfeit.

Bya. Come then, lets see your sister, how she fares now,
After her skirmish: and be sure, *Moroso*   55
Be kept in good hand; then all's perfect, *Livia.*

Exeunt.

Scena quinta.

Enter Jaques and Pedro.

Ped. O *Jaques, Jaques,* what becomes of us?
Oh my sweet Master.

Jaq.   Run for a Physitian,
And a whole peck of Pothecaries, *Pedro.*
He wil die, didle, didle die: if they come not quickly,
And bring all empyricks straight and Mountebankes   5

---

5 empyricks straight and Mountebankes / Skilfull in] MS; people that are
   skilfull / in F1 *

Skilfull in Lungs and Livers: raise the neighbours,
And all the Aquavite-bottles extant;
And, O the Parson, *Pedro*; O the Parson,
A little of his comfort, never so little;
Twenty to one you finde him at the Bush,   10
There's the best Ale.
    Ped.   I fly.

Exit Pedro.

Enter Maria. Servants carrying out household stuff & truncks.

    Mar.   Out with the Trunks, ho:
Why are you idle? Sirha, up to th'Chamber,
And take the hangings down, and see the Linnen
Packt up, and sent away within this halfe houre.
What are the Carts come yet? some honest body   15
Help down the chests of Plate, and some the wardrobe,
Alas we are undone else.
    Jaq.   Pray forsooth,
And I beseech ye, tell me, is he dead yet?
    Mar. No, but is drawing on: out with the Armour.
    Jaq. Then Ile goe see him.
    Mar.   Thou art undone then fellow: 20
No man that has been neere him come neere me.

Enter Sophocles, and Petronius.

    Soph. Why how now Lady, what means this?
    Petron.   Now daughter,
How dos my sonne?
    Mar.   Save all you can for Heavens sake.

Enter Livia, Byancha, and Tranio.

    Liv. Be of good comfort sister.
    Mar.   O my Casket.

11   S.D. *Maria. Servants carrying out houshold stuffe & truncks.*] MS;
      Maria, and Servants. F1 *
23   Heavens] MS, F2; Heaven F1

Petron. How do's thy husband woman?

Mar. Get you gon,   25
If you mean to save your lives: the sicknesse.

Petron. Stand further off, I prethee.

Mar. Is i'th house sir,
My husband has it now;
Alas he is infected, and raves extreamly:
Give me some counsell friends.

Bya. Why lock the doores up,   30
And send him in a woman to attend him.

Mar. I have bespoke two women, and the City
Hath sent a watch by this time: meat nor money
He shall not want, nor prayers.

Petron. How long is't
Since it first tooke him?

Mar. But within this three houres.   35

Enter Watch.

I am frighted from my wits: – – – O here's the watch;
Pray doe your Office, lock the doores up friends,
And patience be his Angel.

They lock the doore.

Tra. This comes unlook'd for:

Mar. Ile to the lodge; some that are kind and love me,
I know wil visit me.

Petruchio within.

Petru. Doe you heare my Masters: 40
Ho, you that locke the doores up.

Petron. Tis his voyce.

Tra. Hold, and let's heare him.

Petru. Wil ye starve me here:
Am I a Traytor, or an Heretick.
Or am I grown infectious?

38 S.D. The lock the doore.] MS; *om.* F1 *

Petron.   Pray sir, pray.

Petru. I am as wel as you are, goodman puppy.   45

Mar. Pray have patience,

You shall want nothing sir.

Petru.   I want a cudgell,

And thee, thou wickednesse.

Petron.   He speakes wel enough.

Mar. 'Had ever a strong heart sir.

Petru.   Wil ye heare me? first be pleas'd

To think I know ye all, and can distinguish   50

Ev'ry mans severall voyce: you that spoke first,

I know my father in law; the other *Tranio*,

And I heard *Sophocles*; the last, pray marke me,

Is my dam'd wife *Maria*: gentlemen,

If any man misdoubt me for infected,   55

There is mine arme, let any man looke on't.

Enter Doctor and Pothecary.

Doct. Save ye Gentlemen.

Petron.   O welcome Doctor,

Ye come in happy time; pray your opinion,

What think you of his pulse?

Doct.   It bears with busiest,

And shews a general inflammation,   60

Which is the symptome of a pestilent feaver,

Take twenty ounces from him.

Petru.   Take a foole;

Take an ounce from mine arme, and Doctor Deuz-ace,

Ile make a close-stoole of your Velvet costard.

Death, gentlemen, doe ye make a may-game on me? 65

I tell ye once againe, I am as sound,

As wel, as wholsome, and as sensible,

As any of ye all: Let me out quickly,

Or as I am a man, Ile beat the wals down,

And the first thing I light upon shall pay for't.   70

54   gentlemen,] MS; *om.* F1 *

65   Death, gentlemen,] MS; ——Gentlemen F1-2

Exit Doctor and Pothecary.

Petro. Nay we'l go with you Doctor.
Mar.   Tis the safest;
I saw the tokens sir.
    Petro.   Then there is but one way.
    Petru. Wil it please you open?
    Tra.   His fit grows stronger still.
    Mar. Let's save our selves sir.
He's past all wordly cure.
    Petro.   Friends do your office.   75
And what he wants, if money, love, or labour,
Or any way may win it, let him have it.
Farewell, and pray my honest friends – – –

Exeunt manent Watchman.

    Petru.   Why Rascals,
Friends, Gentlemen, thou beastly wife, *Jaques*;
None heare me? who's at the doore there?
    1 *Watch.*   Thinke I pray sir,   80
Whether you are going, and prepare your selfe.
    2 *Watch.* These idle thoughts disturbe you, the good
                             Gentlewoman
Your wife has taken care you shall want nothing.
    Petru. The blessing of her grandam Eve light on her,
Nothing but thin fig leaves to hide her knavery.   85
Shall I come out in quiet? answer me,
Or shall I charge a fowling-piece, and make
Mine own way; two of ye I cannot misse,
If I misse three; ye come here to assault me.
    1 *Watch.* There's onions rosting for your sore, Sir.
    Petru.   People   90
I am as excellent wel, I thank Heav'n for't,

78 S.D. *manent Watchmen.*] MS; *om.* F1 *
80 who's] MS; who F1-2
84-85 The blessing . . . her knavery.] MS; *om.* F1 *
90 1. *Watch.* There's onions . . . sore, Sir.] MS; *om.* F1 *
    People,] MS; *om.* F1 *

And have as good a stomacke at this instant – – –
    2 *Watch.*   That's an ill signe.
    1 *Watch.*   He draws on; he's a dead man,
    Petru.   And sleep as soundly; wil ye looke upon me?
    1 *Watch.*   Do you want Pen and Inke? while you have
Settle your state.   [sence sir, 95
    Petru.   Sirs, I am wel, as you are;
Or any Rascall living.
    2 *Watch.*   would you were sir.
    Petru.   Look to your selves, and if you love your lives,
Open the doore, and fly me, for I shoot else;
I sweare Ile shoot, and presently, chain-bullets;   100
And under foure I will not kill.
    1 *Watch.*   Let's quit him,
It may be it is a trick: he's dangerous.
    2 *Watch.*   The devill take the hinmost, I cry.

                 Exit watch running.

    Enter Petruchio with a piece, and forces the doore open.

    Petru.   Have among ye;
The doore shall open too, Ile have a faire shoot;
Are ye all gone? tricks in my old daies, crackers   105
Put now upon me? and by Lady *Green-sleeves*?
Am I grown so tame after all my triumphs?
But that I should be thought mad, if I rail'd
As much as they deserve against these women,
I would now rip up from the primitive cuckold,   110
All their arch-villanies, and all their doubles,
Which are more then a hunted Hare ere thought on:
When a man has the fairest, and the sweetest
Of all their sex, and as he thinks the noblest,
What has he then? and Ile speake modestly,   115
He has a Quartern-ague, that shall shake

100   I sweare Ile] MS; ——Ile F1-2
102   is a trick:] F2; 'tis a trick, MS; is trick: F1
103   S.D. *piece, and forces the doore open.*] MS; *piece.* F1 *

All his estate to nothing; never cur'd,
Nor never dying; H'as a ship to venture
His fame, and credit in, which if he man not
With more continuall labour then a Gally   120
To make her tith, either she grows a Tumbrell
Not worth the cloth she weares; or springs more leakes
Then all the fame of his posterity
Can ever stop againe: out on 'em hedge-hogs,
He that shal touch 'em, has a thousand thorns   125
Runs through his fingers: If I were unmarried,
I would do any thing below repentance,
Any base dunhill slavery; be a hang-man,
Ere I would be a husband: O the thousand,
Thousand, ten thousand waies they have to kil us!   130
Some fall with too much stringing of the Fiddles,
And those are fooles; some, that they are not suffer'd,
And those are Maudlin-lovers: some, like Scorpions,
They poyson with their tailes, and those are Martyrs;
Some die with doing good, those Benefactors,   135
And leave 'em land to leap away: some few,
For those are rarest, they are said to kill
With kindnesse, and faire usage; but what they are   _Irony_
My Catologue discovers not: onely tis thought
They are buried in old wals with their heeles upward.   140
I could raile twenty daies together now.
Ile seek 'em out, and if I have not reason,
And very sensible, why this was done,
Ile go a birding yet, and some shall smart for't.

                    Exit.

---

124   again:] MS; again: I could rail twenty daies; F1; again. I could raile
      twenty dayes; F2

Enter Moroso and Petronius.

Mor. That I do love her, is without all question,
And most extreamly, deerly, most exactly;
And that I would ev'n now, this present Monday
Before all others, maids, wives, women, widdows,
Of what degree or calling, marry her,   5
As certaine too; but to be made a whim-wham,
A Jib-crack, and a Gentleman o'th first house
For all my kindnesse to her.
    Petron.   How you take it?
Thou get a wench, thou get a dozen night-caps;
Wouldst have her come, and lick thee like a calfe,   10
And blow thy nose, and busse thee?
    Mor.   Not so neither.
    Petron. What wouldst thou have her do?
    Mor.   Do as she should do;
Put on a clean smock, and th Church, and marry,
And then to bed a Gods name, this is faire play,
And keeps the Kings peace; let her leave her bobs,   15
I have had too many of them, and her quillets,
She is as nimble that way as an Eele;
But in the way she ought to me especially,
A sow of Lead is swifter.
    Petron.   Quoat your griefes down.
    Mor. Give faire quarter, I am old and crasie,   20

9   get a dozen] F2; get dozen F1

And subject to much fumbling, I confesse it;
Yet something I would have that's warme, to hatch me:
But understand me I would have it so,
I buy not more repentance in the bargaine
Then the ware's worth I have; if you allow me   25
Worthy your Son-in-law, and your allowance,
Do it a way of credit; let me show so,
And not be troubled in my visitations,
With blows, and bitternesse, and down right railings,
As if we were to couple like two cats,   30
With clawing, and loud clamour:
 Petron.   Thou fond man
Hast thou forgot the Ballad, crabbed age,
Can *May* and *Ianuary* match together,
And nev'r a storm between 'em? say she abuse thee,
Put case she doe.
 Mor.   Wel.
 Petron.   Nay, believe she do's.   35
 Mor. I doe believe she do's.
 Petron.   And div'lishly:
Art thou a whit the worse?
 Mor.   That's not the matter,
I know, being old, tis fit I am abus'd;
I know tis hansome, and I know moreover
I am to love her for't.
 Petron.   Now you come to me.   40
 Mor. Nay more then this; I find too, and finde certain,
What Gold I have, Pearle, Bracelets, Rings, or Owches,
Or what she can desire, Gowns, Petticotes,
Wastcotes, Embroydered-stockings, Scarffs, Cals, Feathers
Hats, five pound Garters, Muffs, Masks, Ruffs, & Ribands,   45
I am to give her for't.
 Petron.   Tis right, you are so.
 Mor. But when I have done all this, and think it duty,
Is't requisit an other bore my nostrils?
Riddle me that.

32 Ballad,] F2; Ballard, F1

Petron.   Go get you gone, and dreame
She's thine within these two daies, for she is so;   50
The boy's beside the saddle: get warm broths,
And feed apace; think not of worldly businesse,
It cools the blood; leave off your tricks, they are hateful,
And meere forerunners of the ancient measures;
Contrive your beard o'th top cut like Verdugoes;   55
It shows you would be wise, and burn your night-cap,
It looks like halfe a winding-sheet, and urges
From a young wench nothing but cold repentance:
You may eate Onyons, so you'l not be lavish.
     Mor. I am glad of that.
     Petron.   They purge the blood, and quicken,   60
But after 'em, conceive me, sweep your mouth,
And where there wants a tooth, stick in a clove.
     Mor. Shall I hope once againe, say't.
     Petro.   You shall sir:
And you shall have your hope.

Enter Byancha and Tranio.

     Moro.   Why there's a match then.
     Byan. You shall not finde me wanting, get you gon.   65
Here's the old man, he'l think you are plotting else
Something against his new Sonne.

Exit Tranio.

     Moro.   Fare ye well sir.

Exit Moroso.

     Byan. And ev'ry Buck had his Doe,
And ev'ry Cuckold a Bell at his Toe:
Oh what sport should we have then, then Boyes then,   70
     O what sport should we have then?
     Petro. This is the spirit, that inspires 'em all.
     By. Give you good ev'n.
     Petro.   A word with you Sweet Lady.

63 *Mor.*] F2; *Mar.* F1

By. I am very hasty sir.

Petro.   So you were ever.

By. Well what's your will?

Petro.   Was not your skilfull hand   75
In this last stratagem? were not your mischiefes
Eeking the matter on?

By.   In's shutting up?
Is that it?

Petro. Yes.

By.   Ile tell you.

Petro.   Doe,

By.   And truly.
Good old man, I doe grieve exceeding much,
I feare too much.

Petro.   I am sorry for your heavinesse.   80
Belike you can repent then?

By.   There you are wide too.
Not that the thing was done (conceive me rightly)
Do's any way molest me.

Petro.   What then Lady?

By. But that I was not in't, there's my sorrow, there
Now you understand me, for Ile tell you,   85
It was so sound a peece, and so well carried,
And if you marke the way, so hansomely,
Of such a heigth, and excellence, and art
I have not known a braver, for conceive me,
When the grosse foole her husband would be sick — — —   90

Petro. Pray stay.

By.   Nay, good, your patience: and no sence for't,
Then stept your daughter in.

Petro.   By your appointment.

By. I would it had, on that condition
I had but one halfe smock, I like it so well;
And like an excellent cunning woman, cur'd me   95
One madnesse with an other, which was rare,
And to our weake beleifes, a wonder.

74   you] F2; your F1

Petro.   Hang ye,
For surely, if your husband looke not to ye,
I know what will.
    By.   I humbly thank your worship.
And so I take my leave.
    Petro.   You have a hand I heare too.   100
    By. I have two sir.
    Petro.   In my young daughters businesse.
    By. You will finde there
A fitter hand then mine, to reach her frets,
And play down diddle to her.
    Petro.   I shall watch ye.
    By. Doe.
    Petro. And I shall have justice.
    By.   Where?
    Petro.   That's all one;   105
I shall be with you at a turne hence forward.
    By. Get you a posset too; and so good ev'n sir.

Exeunt.

Scaena Secunda.

Enter Petruchio, Iaques, and Pedro.

    Iaq. And as I told your worship, all the hangings,
Brasse, Pewter, Plate, ev'n to the very pispots.
    Ped. And that that hung for our defence, the Armor,
And the march Beere was going too: Oh *Iaques*
What a sad sight was that?
    Iaq.   Even the two Rundlets,   5
The two that was our hope, of Muskadell,
(Better nev'r tongue tript over) these two Cannons,
To batter brawne withall at Christmas, sir
Ev'n those two lovely twyns, the enemy

Designation *Scaena Secunda.*] Weber; Scaena j.ma MS; *om.* F1-2
2   pispots.] MS; looking-glasses. F1 *

Had almost cut off cleane.

Petru.   Goe trim the house up.   10
And put the things in order as they were.

Exit Ped. and Iaq.

I shall finde time for all this: could I finde her
But constant any way, I had done my businesse;
Were she a whore directly, or a scold,
An unthrift, or a woman made to hate me,   15
I had my wish and knew which way to rayne her:
But while she shewes all these, and all their losses,
A kinde of linsey woolsey, mingled mischiefe
Not to be ghest at, and whether true, or borrowed,
Not certaine neither, what a hap had I,   20

Enter Maria.

And what a tydie fortune, when my fate
Flung me upon this Beare-whelp? here she comes
Now if she have a colour, for the fault is
A cleanly one, upon my conscience
I shall forgive her yet, and finde a something   25
Certaine, I married for: her wit: Ile marke her.

Mar.   Not let his wife come neere him in his sicknes,
Not come to comfort him? she that all lawes
Of heaven and Nations have ordain'd his second,
Is she refus'd? and two old Paradoxes,   30
Peeces of five and fifty, without faith
Clapt in upon him. h'as a little pet,
That all young wives must follow necessary,
Having their Mayden-heads – – –
Petru.   This is an Axiome
I never heard before.
Mar.   Or say rebellion   35
If we durst be so foule, which two faire words
Alas win us from, in an houre, an instant,
We are so easie, make him so forgetfull
Both of his reason, honesty, and credit,

As to deny his wife a visitation?   40
His wife, that (though she was a little foolish,)
Lov'd him, Oh heaven forgive her for't! nay doted,
Nay had run mad, had she not married him,
   Petru. Though I doe know this falser then the devill,
I cannot choose but love it.
     Mar.   What doe I know   45
But those that came to keepe him, might have kill'd him,
In what a case had I been then? I dare not
Beleeve him such a base, debosh'd companion,
That one refusall of a tender maide
Would make him faigne this sicknesse out of need,   50
And take a Keeper to him of fourescore
To play at Billiards; one that mew'd content
And all her teeth together; not come neere him?
   Petru. This woman would have made a most rare Jesuite
She can prevaricate on any thing: 55
There was not to be thought a way to save her
In all imagination, beside this.
   Mar. His unkinde dealing, which was worst of all,
In sending, heaven knowes whether, all the plate,
And all the houshold-stuffe, had I not crost it,   60
By a great providence, and my friends assistance
Which he will thanke me one day for: alas,
I could have watch'd as well as they, have serv'd him
In any use, better, and willinger.
The Law commands me to doe it, love commands me,   65
And my own duty charges me.
   Petru.   Heav'n blesse me.
And now I have said my Prayers, Ile goe to her:
Are you a wife for any man?
     Mar.   For you Sir.
If I were worse, I were better; That you are well,
At least, that you appeare so, I thanke heaven,   70
Long may it hold and that you are here, I am glad too,
But that you have abus'd me wretchedly,

And such a way that shames the name of husband,
Such a malicious mangy way, so mingled,
(Never looke strangely on me, I dare tell you)   75
With breach of honesty, care, kindnesse, manners.
    Petru. Holla, you kick too fast.
    Mar.   Was I a stranger?
Or had I vow'd perdition to your person?
Am I not married to you, tell me that?
    Petru. I would I could not tell you.
    Mar.   Is my presence,   80
The stock I come of, which is worshipfull,
If I should say right worshipfull, I ly'd not,
My Grandsire was a Knight.
    Petru.   O'the Shire?
    Mar.   A Souldier,
Which none of all thy Family e're heard off,
But one conductor of thy name, a Grasier   85
That ran away with pay: or am I grown
(Because I have been a little peevish to you,
Onely to try your temper) such a dog-leech
I could not be admitted to your presence?
    Petru. If I endure this, hang me.
    Mar.   And two deaths heads,   90
Two *Harry* Groats, that had their faces worne,
Almost their names away too.
    Petru.   Now heare me.
For I will stay no longer.
    Mar.   This you shall:
However you shall think to flatter me,
For this offence, which no submission   95
Can ever mediate for, you'l finde it so,
What ever you shall doe by intercession,
What you can offer, what your Land can purchase,
What all your friends, or families can win,
Shall be but this, not to forsweare your knowledge,   100
But ever to forbeare it: now your will sir.

88 dog-leech] MS, F2; dogge-latch F1

Petru. Thou art the subtlest woman I think living,
I am sure the lewdest; now be still, and marke me;
Were I but any way addicted to the devill,
I should now think I had met a play-fellow   105
To profit by, and that way the most learned
That ever taught to murmur. Tell me thou,
Thou most poor, paltry spitefull whore: doe you cry?
Ile make you roare, before I leave.
    Mar.   Your pleasure.
    Petru. Was it not sinne enough, thou Fruiterer   110
Full of the fall thou eat'st: thou devils broker,
Thou Seminary of all sedition,
Thou sword of veng'ance, with a thred hung o're us,
Was it not sinne enough, and wickednes
In full abundance? was it not vexation   115
At all points, cap a pe? nay, I shall pinch you,
Thus like a rotten rascall to abuse
The name of heaven, the tye of marriage,
The honour of thy friends; the expectation
Of all that thought thee vertuous, with rebellion,   120
Childish and base rebellion, but continuing
After forgivenesse too, and worse, your mischiefe,
And against him, setting the hope of heaven by,
And the deere reservation of his honour
Nothing above ground could have won to hate thee: 125
Well goe thy wayes.
    Mar.   Yes.
    Petru.   You shall heare me out first:
What punishment mai'st thou deserve, thou thing,
Thou idle thing of nothing, thou pull'd Primrose,
That two houres after, art a weed, and wither'd,
For this last flourish on me? am I one   130
Selected out of all the husbands living,
To be so ridden by a Tit of ten pence,
Am I so blind and Bed-rid? I was mad,
And had the Plague, and no man must come neere me,
I must be shut up, and my substance bezel'd,   135

And an old woman watch me.
  Mar.   Well sir, well,
You may well glory in't.
  Petru. And when it comes to opening, 'tis my plot,
I must undoe my selfe forsooth: do'st heare me?
If I should beat thee now, as much may be,   140
Do'st thou not well deserve it, o' thy conscience,
Do'st thou not cry, come beat me?
  Mar.   I defie you.
And my last loving teares farwell: the first stroke,
The very first you give me, if you dare strike,
Try me, and you shall finde it so, for ever   145
Never to be recall'd: I know you love me,
Mad till you have enjoy'd me; I doe turne
Utterly from you, and what man I meet first
That has but spirit to deserve a favour,
Let him beare any shape, the worse the better,   150
Shall kill you, and enjoy me; what I have said
About your foolish sicknesse, e're you have me
As you would have me, you shall sweare, is certaine,
And challenge any man, that dares deny it;
And in all companies approve my actions,   155
And so farwell for this time.

Exit Mar.

  Petru.   Grief goe with thee,
If there be any witchcrafts, herbes, or potions,
Saying my Prayers back-ward, Fiends, or Fayries
That can againe unlove me, I am made.

Exit.

Scaena tertia.

Enter Byancha, and Tranio.

  Tra. Faith Mistresse, you must doe it.

Designation *Scaena Tertia.*] Weber; *om.* MS; *Scaena Secunda.* F1-2
1 Faith] MS; *om.* F1 *

By. Are the writings ready I told you of?

Tra. Yes they are ready, but to what use I know not.

By. Y'are an Asse, you must have all things constru'd,

Tra. Yes, and peirc'd too,   5
Or I finde little pleasure.

By.   Now you are knavish,
Goe too, fetch *Rowland* hither presently,
Your twenty pound lies bleeding else: she is married
Within these twelve houres, if we crosse it not,
And see the Papers of one size.

Tra.   I have ye.   10

By. And for disposing of 'em.

Tra.   If I faile you
Now I have found the way, use Marshall Law
And cut my head off with a hand Saw:

By.   Wel sir.
Petronius and *Moroso* I'le see sent for
About your businesse; goe.

Tra.   I am gone.

Exit Tra.
Enter Livia.

By.   Ho *Livia.*   15

Liv. Who's that?

By.   A friend of yours, Lord how you looke now,
As if you had lost a Carrick.

Liv.   O *Byancha.*
I am the most undone, unhappy woman.

By. Be quiet wench, thou shalt be done, and done,
And done, and double done, or all shall split for't,   20
No more of these minc'd passions, they are mangy,
And ease thee of nothing, but a little wind,
An apple will doe more: thou fear'st *Moroso.*

Liv. Even as I feare the Gallowes.

By.   Keepe thee there still.
And you love *Rowland?* say.

Liv.   If I say not   25

I am sure I lye.

By.　　　　What would'st thou give that woman,
In spight of all his anger, and thy feare,
And all thy Fathers policy, that could
Clap ye within these two nights quietly
Into a Bed together?

Liv.　　　　How?

By.　　　　　　Why fairely,　　　　　　　　30
At half sword man and wife: now the red blood comes,
I marry now the matters chang'd.

Liv.　　　　　　*Byancha,*
Me thinks you should not mock me.

By.　　　　　　　Mock a pudding.
I speake good honest English, and good meaning.

Liv. I should not be ungratefull to that woman.　　35

By. I know thou would'st not, follow but my Councell
And if thou hast him not, despight of fortune
Let me nev'r know a good night more; you must
Be very sick o'th instant.

Liv.　　　　Well, what follows?

By. And in that sicknesse send for all your friends,　　40
Your Father, and your feavor old *Moroso,*
And *Rowland* shall be there too.

Liv.　　　　　　What of these?

By. Doe you not twitter yet? of this shall follow
That which shall make thy heart leape, and thy lips
Venture as many kisses, as the Merchants　　　　45
Doe dollars to the East-Indies: you shall know all,
But first walke in, and practice, pray be sick.

Liv. I doe beleeve you: and I am sick.

By.　　　　　　Doe
To bed then, come, Ile send away your Servants
Post for your Foole, and Father; and good fortune,　　50
As we meane honesty, now strike an up-shot.

Exeunt.

Scaena Quarta.

Enter Tranio, and Rowland.

Tra. Nay, on my conscience, I have lost my money,
But that's all one: Ile never more perswade you,
I see you are resolute, and I commend you.
    Row. But did she send for me?
    Tra.   You dare beleeve me.
    Row. I cannot tell, you have your waies for profit   5
Allow'd you *Tranio*, as well as I
Have to avoid 'em feare:
    Tra.   No, on my word sir
I deale directly with you.

Enter Servant.

    Row.   How now fellow,
Whither Post you so fast?
    Serv.   O sir my Master
Pray did you see my Master?
    Row.   Why your Master?   10
    Serv. Sir his Jewell.
    Row.   With the gilded Button?
    Serv. My pretty Mistresse *Livia.*
    Row.   What of her?
    Serv. Is falne sick o'th suddaine.
    Row.   How o'th sullens?
    Serv. O'th suddaine sir, I say, very sick:
    Row. It seemes she hath got the toothach with raw apples.   15
    Serv. It seemes you have got the headach, fare you well sir.
You did not see my Master?
    Row.   Who told you so?
    Tra. No, no, he did not see him.
    Row.   Farewell blew bottle.

Exit Servant.

What should her sicknesse be?

Designation *Scaena Quarta.*] Weber; *om.* MS; *Scaena Tertia* F1-2

Tra.   For you it may be.

Row.   Yes when my braines are out, I may beleeve it,   20
Never before I am sure: yet I may see her
'Twill be a point of honesty:

Tra.   It will so.

Row.   It may be not too: you would faine be fingring
This old sinne-offring of two hundred, *Tranio,*
How daintily, and cunningly you drive me   25
Up like a Deere to'th toyle, yet I may leape it,
And what's the woodman then?

Tra.   A looser by you.
Speake will you go or not? to me 'tis equall.

Row.   Come what goes lesse?

Tra.   Nay not a penny *Rowland.*

Row.   Shall I have liberty of conscience   30
Which by interpretation, is ten kisses?
Hang me if I affect her: yet it may be,
This whorson manners will require a strugling,
Of two and twenty, or by'r-Lady thirty.

Tra.   By'r-lady Ile require my wager then,   35
For if you kisse so often, and no kindnesse,
I have lost my speculation, i'le allow you – – –

Row.   Speake like a Gamster now.

Tra.   It may be two.

Row.   Under a dozen *Tranio*, ther's no setting,
You shall have forty shillings, winck at small faults.   40
Say I take twenty, come, by all that's honest
I doe it but to vex her.

Tra.   Ile no by-blowes.
If you can love her doe, if you can, hate her,
Or any else that loves you.

Row.   Prethee *Tranio.*

Tra.   Why farewell twenty pound, twill not undoe me;   45
You have my resolution.

Row.   And your money,

42   by-blowes.] MS, F2; by-lowes. F1
43   you can,] F2; ye can MS; ~ ~ F1

Which since you are so stubborne, if I forfeit,
Make me a Jack o' Lent, and breake my shins
For untag'd points and Compters: Ile goe with you,
But if thou gett'st a penny by the bargaine;   50
A parting kisse is lawfull?
    Tra.   I allow it.
    Row. Knock out my braines with Apples; yet a bargaine:
    Tra. I tell you, i'le no bargaines; win, and weare it.
    Row. Thou art the strangest fellow.
    Tra.   That's all one.
    Row. Along then, twenty pound more if thou dar'st,   55
I give her not a good word.
    Tra.   Not a Penny.

Exeunt.

Scaena Quinta.

Enter Petruchio, Jaques, and Pedro.

    Petru. Prethee, entreat her come, I will not trouble her
Above a word or two; ere I endure

Exit Pedro.

This life, and with a woman, and a vow'd one
To all the mischiefes she can lay upon me,
Ile goe to Plough again, and eat leeke Porridge;   5
Begging's a pleasure to't not to be numberd:
No there be other Countries *Iaques* for me,
And other people, yea, and other women.
If I have need, here's money, there's your ware,
Which is faire dealing, and the Sunne, they say   10
Shines as warme there, as here, and till I have lost
Either my selfe, or her, I care not whether
Nor which first.
    Iaq.   Will your worship heare me?

48   my shins] MS, F2; shins F1

Petru. And utterly outworne the memory
Of such a curse as this, none of my Nation   15
Shall ever know me more.
    Iaq.   Out alas sir
What a strange way doe you runne?
    Petru.   Any way,
So I out-runne this rascall.
    Iaq.   Me thinkes now,
If your good worship could but have the patience.
    Petru. The patience, why the patience?
    Iaq.   Why i'le tell you,   20
Could you but have the patience.
    Petru.   Well the patience.
    Iaq. To laugh at all she do's, or when she railes,
To have a drum beaten o'th top o'th house,
To give the neighbours warning of her Larme,
As I doe when my wife rebels.
    Petru.   Thy wife?   25
Thy wife's a Pigeon to her a meere slumber,
The dead of night's not stiller.
    Iaq.   Nor an Iron Mill.
    Petru. But thy wife is certaine.
    Iaq.   That's false Doctrine,
You never read of a certaine woman.
    Petru. Thou know'st her way.
    Ja.   I should doe, I am sure.   30
I have ridden it night, and day, this twenty yeare.
    Petru. But mine is such a drench of Balderdash,
Such a strange carded cunningnesse, the Rayne-bow
When she hangs bent in heaven, sheds not her colours
Quicker and more then this deceitfull woman   35

Enter Ped.

Weaves in her dyes of wickednesse: what sayes she?
    Ped. Nay not a word sir, but she pointed to me,
As though she meant to follow; pray sir bear it
Ev'n as you may, I need not teach your worship,

The best men have their crosses, we are all mortall.   40
    Petru. What ailes the fellow?
    Ped.   And no doubt she may sir
    Petru. What may she, or what do's she, or what is she?
Speake and be hang'd.
    Ped.   She's mad Sir.
    Petru.   Heaven continue it.
    Ped. Amen if't be his pleasure.
    Petru.   How mad is she?
    Ped. As mad as heart can wish sir: she has drest her self   45
(Saving your worships reverence) just i'th cut
Of one of those that multiply i'th Suburbs
For single money, and as durtily:
If any speake to her, first she whistles,
And then begins her compasse with her fingers,   50
And points to what she would have.
    Petru.   What new waye's this?
    Ped. There came in Master *Sophocles*,
    Petru.   And what
Did Master *Sophocles* when he came in?
Get my Truncks ready sirha, i'le be gone straight.
    Ped. He's here to tell you   55

Enter Sophocles.

She's horne mad *Iaques.*
    Soph.   Call ye this a woman?
    Petru. Yes sir, she is a woman,
    Soph.   Sir, I doubt it.
    Petru. I had thought you had made experience,
    Soph.   Yes I did so.
And almost with my life.
    Petru.   You rid too fast sir.
    Soph. Pray be not mistaken: by this hand   60
Your wife's as chaste, and honest as a virgin,
For anything I know: 'tis true she gave me
A Ring.

58   made] MS, F2; make F1

Petru.   For rutting.

Soph.   You are much deceiv'd still,

Beleeve me, I never kist her since, and now

Coming in visitation, like a friend,   65

I thinke she is mad sir, suddainly she started,

And snatch'd the Ring away, and drew her knife out,

To what intent I know not.

Petru.   Is this certaine?

Soph.   As I am here sir.

Petru.   I beleeve you honest.

             Enter Maria.

And pray continue so.

Soph.   She comes.

Petru.   Now Damsell,   70

What will your beauty doe, if I forsake you?

Doe you deale by signes, and tokens? as I ghesse then,

You'l walke abroad, this Sommer, and catch Captaines,

Or hire a peece of holy ground i'th Suburbs,

And keepe a neast of Nuns?   *whores*

Soph.   O doe not stir her!   75

You see in what a case she is?

Petru.   She is dogged,

And in a beastly case I am sure: Ile make her

If she have any tongue, yet tatle. *Sophocles*

Prethee observe this woman seriously,

And eye her well, and when thou hast done, but tell me   80

(For thou hast understanding) in what case

My sence was, when I chose this thing.

Soph.   Ile tell you

I have seene a sweeter – – –

Petru.   An hundred times cry oysters.

Ther's a poore Begger wench about Black-Fryers

Runs on her breech may be an Empresse to her.   85

Soph.   Nay, now you are too bitter.

Petru.   Nev'r a whit sir:

Ile tell thee woman; for now I have day to see thee,

And all my wits about me, and I speake
Not out of passion neither (leave your mumping)
I know you're well enough: Now would I give   90
A million but to vex her: when I chose thee
To make a Bedfellow, I tooke more trouble,
Then twenty Termes can come too, such a cause,
Of such a title, and so everlasting
That *Adams* Genealogie may be ended   95
Ere any law find thee: I tooke a Leprosie,
Nay worse, the plague, nay worse yet, a possession
And had the devill with thee, if not more:
And yet worse, was a beast, and like a beast
Had my reward, a Jade to fling my fortunes;   100
For who that had but reason to distinguish
The light from darknesse, wine from water, hunger
From full satiety, and Fox from ferne bush
That would have married thee?
    Soph.   She is not so ill.
    Petru. She's worse then I dare think of: she's so lewd,   105
No Court is strong enough to bear her cause,
She hath neither manners, honesty, behavour,
Wife-hood, nor woman-hood, nor any morall
Can force me think she had a mother, no
I do believe her stedfastly, and know her   110
To be a woman-Woolfe by transmigration,
Her first forme was a Ferrets undergrounde,
She kils the memories of men: not yet?
    Soph. Do you think she's sensible of this?
    Petru.   I care not,
Be what she will: the pleasure I take in her,   115
Thus I blow off; the care I took to love her,
Like this point I unty, and thus I loose it,
The husband I am to her, thus I sever:
My vanity farwell: yet, for you have bin
So neer me as to bear the name of wife,   120
My unquench'd charity shall tell you thus much
(Though you deserve it well) you shall not beg,

What I ordan'd your Jointure, honestly
You shall have setled on you: and half my house,
the other half shall be imploy'd in prayers,   125
(That meritorious charge Ile be at also
Yet to confirm you christian) your apparrell,
And what belongs to build up such a folly,
Keep I beseech you, it infects our uses,
And now I am for travell.
    Mar.   Now I love you,   130
And now I see you are a man ile talk to you,
And I forget your bitternesse.
    Soph.   How now man?
    Petru. O *Pliny*, if thou wilt be ever famous
Make but this woman all thy wonders.
    Mar.   Sure sir
You have hit upon a happy course, a blessed,   135
And what will make you vertuous?
    Petru.   She'l ship me.
    Mar. A way of understanding I long wishd for,
And now tis come, take heed you fly not back sir,
Me thinks you look a new man to me now,
A man of excellence, and now I see   140
Some great design set in you: you may think now
(And so may most that know me) 'twere my part
Weakly to weep your losse, and to resist you,
Nay hang about your neck and like a dotard
Urge my strong tie upon you: but I love you,   145
And all the world shall know it, beyond woman,
And more prefer the honour of your Country,
Which chiefly you are born for, and may perfect,
The uses you may make of other Nations,
The ripening of your knowledge, conversation,   150
The full ability, and strength of judgement,
Then any private love, or wanton kisses.
Go worthy man, and bring home understanding.
    Soph. This were an excellent woman to breed School-men.
    Mar. For if the Merchant through unknown Seas plough   155

To get his wealth, then deer sir, what must you
To gather wisdom? go, and go alone,
Only your noble mind for your companion,
And if a woman may win credit with you,
Go far: too far you cannot: still the farther   160
The more experience finds you: and go sparing,
One meale a week will serve you, and one sute,
Through all your travels: for you'l find it certaine,
The poorer and the baser you appear,
The more you look through still.

    Petru.   Do'st hear her?
    Soph.   Yes.   165
    Petru. What would this woman do if she were suffer'd,
Upon a new religion?
    Soph.   Make us Pagans,
I wonder that she writes not.
    Mar.   Then when time,
And fulnesse of occasion have new made you,
And squard you from a sot into a Signour,   170
Or neere from a lade into a courser;
Come home an aged man, as did *Ulysses*,
And I your glad *Penelope*.
    Petru.   That must have
As many lovers as I languages,
And what she do's with one i'th day, i'th night   175
Undoe it with an other.
    Mar.   Much that way sir;
For in your absence, it must be my honour,
That, that must make me spoken of hereafter,
To have temptations, and not little ones
Daily and hourely offer'd me, and strongly,   180
Almost believed against me, to set off
The faith, and loyalty of her that loves you.
    Petru. What should I do?

---

167 religion?] MS, F2; adventure F1
    Pagans,] MS, F2; nothing, F1

Soph.   Why by my troth, I would travell,
Did not you mean so?
  Petru.   Alas no, nothing lesse man:
I did it but to try her, shee's the devill,   185
And now I find it, for she drives me, I must go:
Are my trunks down there, and my horses ready?
  Mar. Sir, for your house, and if you please to trust me
With that you leave behinde.
  Petru.   Bring down the money.
  Mar. As I am able, and to my poor fortunes,   190
I'le govern as a widow: I shall long
To hear of your wel-doing, and your profit:
And when I hear not from you once a quarter,
I'le wish you in the Indies, or Cataya,
Those are the climes must make you.
  Petru.   How's the wind?   195
She'l wish me out o'th world anon.
  Mar.   For France.
Tis very faire; get you aboard to night sir,
And loose no time, you know the tide staies no man,
I have cold meats ready for you.
  Petru.   Far thee well,
Thou hast foold me o'th Kingdom with a vengeance,   200
And thou canst foole me in againe.
  Mar.   Not I sir,
I love you better, take your time, and pleasure,
Ile see you hors'd.
  Petru.   I think thou wouldst see me hangd too,
Were I but halfe as willing.
  Mar.   Any thing
That you think well of, I dare look upon.   205
  Petru. You'l bear me to the lands end *Sophocles*,
And other of my friends I hope.
  Mar.   Nev'r doubt sir,
You cannot want companions for your good:

183   my troth,] MS; my—— F1-2
185   try her] MS; try sir, F1; try, sir F2

I am sure you'l kisse me ere I go; I have businesse,
And stay long here I must not.
    Petru.   Get thee going.   210
For if thou tarriest but an other Dialogue
Ile kick thee to thy Chamber.
    Mar.   Fare you well Sir,
And bear your selfe, I do beseech you once more,
Since you have undertaken doing wisely,
Manly, and worthily, tis for my credit,   215
And for those flying fames here of your follies,
Your gambols, and ill breeding of your youth,
For which I understand you take this travell,
Nothing should make me leave you els, ile deale
So like a wife, that loves your reputation,   220
And the most large addition of your credit,
That those shall die: if you want Limon-waters,
Or any thing to take the edge o'th Sea off,
Pray speak, and be provided.
    Petru.   Now the Devill,
That was your first good master, shoure his blessing   225
Upon ye all: into whose custody – – –
    Mar. I do commit your Reformation,
And so I leave you to your *Stilo novo.*

Exit Maria.

    Petru. I will go: yet I will not: once more *Sophocles*
Ile put her to the test.
    Soph.   You had better go.   230
    Petru. I will go then: let's seek my father out,
And all my friends to see me faire aboard:
Then women, if there be a storme at Sea,
Worse then your tongues can make, and waves more broken
Then your dissembling fayths are, let me feele   235
Nothing but tempests, till they crack my Keele.

Exeunt.

Enter Petronius, and Byancha with foure papers.

By. Now whether I deserve that blame you gave me,
Let all the world discern sir.
    Petron.   If this motion,
(I mean this fair repentance of my Daughter)
Spring from your good perswasion, as it seems so,
I must confesse I have spoke too boldly of you,   5
And I repent.
    By.   The first touch was her own,
Taken no doubt from disobeying you,
The second I put to her, when I told her
How good, and gentle yet, with free contrition
Again you might be purchas'd: loving woman,   10
She heard me, and I thank her, thought me worthy
Observing in this point: yet all my councell,
And comfort in this case, could not so heal her
but that grief got his share too, and she sickend.
    Petron. I am sorry she's so ill, yet glad her sicknesse   15
Has got so good a ground.

Enter Moroso.

    By.   here comes *Moroso.*
    Petron. O you are very welcome,
Now you shall know your happinesse.
    Mor.   I am glad on't.
What makes this Lady here?

By.   A dish for you sir
You'l thank me for hereafter.
Petron.   True *Moroso*,   20
Go get you in, and see your Mistris.
By.   She is sick sir,
But you may kisse her whole.
Mor.   How?
By.   Comfort her.
Mor. Why am I sent for sir?
Petron.   Will you in, and see?
By. May be she needs confession.
Mor.   By St. *Mary*,
She shall have absolution then and pennance,   25
But not above her carriage.
Petron.   Get you in foole.

Exit Mor.

By. Here comes the other too.

En. Rowland and Tranio.

Petron.   Now *Tranio*.
Good ev'n to you too, and you are welcome.
Row. Thank you.
Petron.   I have a certaine Daughter.
Row.   Would you had sir.
Petron. No doubt you know her well.
Row.   Nor never shall sir.   30
She is a woman, and the waies unto her
Are like the finding of a certaine path
After a deep falne Snow.
Petron.   Well thats byth' by still.
This Daughter that I tell you of is falne
A little crop sick, with the dangerous surfeit   35
She took of your affection.
Row.   Mine sir?
Petron.   Yes sir.
Or rather, as it seemes, repenting.

And there she lies within, debating on't,

 Row.   Well sir.

 Petron. I think 'twere well you would see her.

 Row.   If you please sir;

I am not squeamish of my visitation.   40

 Petron. But, this ile tell you, she is alter'd much,

You'l finde her now an other *Livia*.

 Row. I have enough o'th old sir.

 Petron.   No more foole,

To look gay babies in your eyes yong *Rowland*,

And hang about your prety neck.

 Row.   I am glad on't,   45

And thank my Fates I have scapd such execution.

 Petron. And busse you till you blush againe.

 Row.   Thats hard sir,

She must kisse shamefully ere I blush at it,

I never was so boyish; well, what followes?

 Petron. She's mine now, as I please to settle her,   50

At my command, and where I please to plant her:

Only she would take a kind of farwell of you,

And give you back a wandring vow or two,

You left in pawn; and two or three slight oaths

She lent you too, she looks for.

 Row.   She shall have 'em   55

With all my heart sir, and if you like it better,

A free release in writing.

 Petron.   Thats the matter,

And you from her, you shall have an other *Rowland*,

And then turne taile to taile, and peace be with you.

 Row. So be it: your twenty pound sweats *Tranio*.   60

 Tra. 'Twill not undoe me *Rowland*, do your worst.

 Row. Come, shall we see her Sir?

 By.   What ere she saies

You must beare manly *Rowland*, for her sicknesse

Has made her somewhat teatish.

 Row.   Let her talke

Till her tongue ake I care not: by this hand   65

Thou hast a handsome face wench, and a body
Daintely mounted; now do I feele an hundred
Running directly from me, as I pist it.

Enter Livia discovered abed, and Moroso by her.

By. Pray draw 'em softly, the least hurry sir
Puts her to much impatience.
 Petron.   How is't daughter?   70
 Liv. O very sick, very sick, yet somewhat
Better I hope; a little lightsommer,
Because this goodman has forgiven me;
Pray set me higher; Oh my head:
 Bya.   Wel done wench.
 Liv. Father, and all good people that shal heare me, 75
I have abus'd this man perniciously;
Was never old man humbled so; I have scornd him,
And cal'd him nasty names, I have spit at him,
Flung Candles ends in's beard, and cald him harrow,
That must be drawn to all he dos: contemn'd him, 80
For me thought then he was a beastly fellow.
(Oh God my side) a very beastly fellow:
And gave it out, his cassock was a Barge-cloth,
Pawnd to his predecessor by a Sculler,
The man yet living: I gave him purging-comfits 85
At a great christning once,
That spoyl'd his Chamblet breeches; and one night
I strewd the staires with pease, as he past down;
And the good Gentleman (woe worth me for't)
Ev'n with this reverent head, this head of wisdome, 90
Told two and twenty staires, good and true;
Mist not a step, and as we say verbatim
Fell to the bottome, broke his casting Bottle,
Lost a fair toad-stone of some eighteen shillings,
Jumbled his joynts together, had two stooles, 95
And was translated. All this villany
Did I: I *Livia*, I alone, untaught.

90 this reverent] MS, F2; his reverent F1

Mor. And I unask'd, forgive it.

Liv.   Where's *Byancha*?

Bya. Here Cozen.

Liv.   Give me drinke,

Bya.   There.

Liv.   Who's that?

Mor.   *Rowland.*

Liv. O'my dissembler, you and I must part.   100
Come neerer sir.

Row.   I am sorry for your sicknesse.

Liv. Be sorry for your selfe sir, you have wrong'd me,
But I forgive you; are the papers ready?

Bya. I have 'em here: wilt please you view 'em?

Petron.   Yes.

Liv. Shew 'em the young man too, I know he's willing   105
To shift his sailes too: tis for his more advancement;
Alas, we might have beggerd one another;
We are young both, and a world of children
Might have been left behind to curse our follies:
We had been undone *Byancha*, had we married,   110
Undone for ever: I confesse I lov'd him,
I care not who shall know it, most intirely;
And once, upon my conscience, he lov'd me;
But farewell that, we must be wiser cosen.
Love must not leave us to the world: have you done?   115

Row. Yes, and am ready to subscribe.

Liv.   Pray stay then:
Give me the papers, and let me peruse 'em,
And so much time, as may afford a teare
At our last parting.

Bya.   Pray retire, and leave her,
Ile call ye presently.

Petro.   Come Gentlemen,   120
The showre must fall.

Row.   Would I had never seen her.

---

121   S.D. *Exeunt all, but Bianc. & Livia.*] MS; *om.* F1; *Exeunt* F2

Exeunt all, but Bianc. & Livia.

Bya. Thou hast done bravely wench.

Liv.   Pray Heaven it prove so.

Bya. There are the other papers: when they come
Begin you first, and let the rest subscribe
Hard by your side; give 'em as little light   125
As Drapers doe their wares.

Liv.   Didst mark *Moroso*,
In what an agony he was, and how he cry'd most
When I abus'd him most?

Bya.   That was but reason.

Liv. Oh what a stinking thief is this?
Though I was but to counterfeit, he made me   130
Directly sick indeed. Tames-street to him
Is a meere Pomander.

Bya. Let him be hang'd.

Liv.   Amen.

Bya.   And lie you still.
And once more to your businesse.

Liv.   Call 'em in.
Now if there be a power that pities lovers,   135
Helpe now, and heare my prayers.

Enter Petronius, Rowland, Tranio, Moroso.

Petro.   Is she ready?

Bya. She has done her lamentations: pray go to her.

Liv. *Rowland*, come neer me, and before you seale,
Give me your hand: take it again; now kisse me,
This is the last acquaintance we must have;   140
I wish you ever happy: there's the paper.

Row. Pray stay a little.

Petro.   Let me never live more
But I do begin to pity this young fellow;
How heartily he weeps!

Bya.   There's Pen and Inke sir.

Liv. Ev'n here I pray you. Tis a little Emblem   145
How neere you have been to me.

Row.   There.

Bya.   Your hands too,

As witnesses.

Petro.   By any means

To th' booke sonne.

Mor.   With all my heart.

Bya.   You must deliver it.

Row. There *Livia*, and a better love light on thee,

I can no more.

Bya.   To this you must be witnesse too.   150

Petro. We wil.

Bya.   Doe you deliver it now.

Lyv.   Pray set me up;

There *Rowland*, all thy old love back: and may

A new to come exceed mine, and be happy.

I must no more.

Row.   Farewell:

Liv.   A long farewell.

Exit Rowl.

Bya. Leave her by any means, till this wild passion   155

Be off her head; draw all the Curtaines close,

A day hence you may see her, twil be better,

She is now for little company.

Petro.   Pray tend her.

I must to horse straight: you must needs along too,

To see my sonne aboard; were but his wife   160

As fit for pity, as this wench, I were happy.

Bya. Time must do that too: fare ye wel; tomorrow

You shall receive a wife to quit your sorrow.

Exeunt.

Scaena secunda.

Enter Jaques, Pedro, and Porters, with Chest and Hampers.

Jaq. Bring 'em away sirs.

Ped.   Must the great Trunks go too?
Jaq.   Yes, and the Hampers; nay be speedy Masters;
He'l be at Sea before us else.
Ped.   O *Jaques,*
What a most blessed turn hast thou?
Jaq.   I hope so.
Ped.   To have the Sea between thee and this woman,   5
Nothing can drown her tongue, but a storm.
Jaq.   By your leave,
We'l get us up to *Paris* with all speed;
For on my soule, as far as *Amyens*
She'l carry blanke; away to Lyon key
And ship 'em presently, we'l follow ye.   10
Ped.   Now could I wish her in that Trunk:
Jaq.   God shield man,
I had rather have a Beare in't.
Ped.   Yes, Ile tell ye:
For in the passage if a Tempest take ye,
As many doe, and you lie beating for it,
Then, if it pleas'd the fates, I would have the Master   15
Out of a powerfull providence, to cry,
Lighten the ship of all hands, or we perish;
Then this for one, as best spar'd, should by all means
Over-board presently.
Jaq.   O' that condition,
So we were certaine to be rid of her,   20
I would wish her with us: But believe me *Pedro,*
She would spoyle the fishing on this coast for ever,
For none would keepe her company, but Dog-fish,
As currish as her selfe; or Porpisces,
Made to all fatal uses: The two Fish-streets   25
Were she but once ariv'd amongst the Whitings,
Would sing a wofull *misereri Pedro,*
And mourn in poor *John,* till her memory
Were cast o'shore agen, with a strong Sea-breach:
She would make god *Neptune,* and his fire-forke,   30
And all his demi-gods, and goddesses,

As weary of the Flemmish channell *Pedro*,
As ever boy was of the schoole: tis certain,
If she but meet him faire, and were wel angred,
She would break his god-head.

Ped.   Oh her tongue, her tongue.   35
Jaq. Rather her many tongues.
Ped.   Or rather strange tongues.
Jaq. Her lying tongue.
Ped.   Her lisping tongue.
Jaq.   Her long tongue.
Ped. Her lawlesse tongue.
Jaq.   Her loud tongue.
Ped.   And her lickrish – –
Jaq. Many other tongues, and many stranger tongues
Then ever Babel had to tell his ruines,   40
Were women rais'd withall; but never a true one.

Enter Sophocles.

Soph. Home with your stuffe agen; the journey's ended.
Jaq. What do's your worship meane?
Soph. Your Master, O *Petruchio*, O poore fellows.
Ped. O *Jaques, Jaques.*
Soph.   O your Master's dead,   45
His body comming back; his wife, his devil;
The griefe of her – – –
Jaq.   Has kild him?
Soph.   Kild him, kild him.
Ped. Is there no law to hang her.
Soph.   Get ye in,
And let her know her misery, I dare not
For feare impatience seize me, see her more,   50
I must away agen: Bid her for wife-hood,
For honesty, if she have any in her,
Even to avoyd the shame that follows her.
Cry if she can: your weeping cannot mend it.
The body wil be here within this houre, so tell her;   55
And all his friends to curse her. Farewell fellowes.

Exit Soph.

Ped. O *Jaques, Jaques.*

Jaq.   O my worthy Master.

Ped. O my most beastly Mistris, hang her.

Jaq.   Split her.

Ped. Drown her directly.

Jaq.   Starve her.

Ped.   Stinke upon her.

Jaq. Stone her to death: may all she eate be Eggs,   60
Till she run kicking mad for men.

   Ped.   And he,
That man, that gives her remedy, pray Heav'n
He may ev'n *ipso facto*, lost his fadings.

   Jaq. Let's goe discharge our selves, and he that serves her,
Or speaks a good word of her from this houre,   65
A Sedgly curse light on him, which is, *Pedro*;
The feind ride through him booted, and spurd, with a Sythe at's
                                                    [back.

Exeunt.

Scena tertia.

Enter Rowland, and Tranio stealing behind him.

   Row. What a dull asse was I to let her go thus?
Upon my life she loves me still: wel Paper,
Thou onely monument of what I have had,
Thou all the love now left me, and now lost,
Let me yet kisse her hand, yet take my leave   5
Of what I must leave ever: Farewell *Livia.*
Oh bitter words, Ile read ye once again,
And then for ever study to forget ye.
How's this? let me look better on't: A Contract?
I sweare a Contract, seal'd, and ratified,   10

63   fadings.] MS; longings. F1; Fadding F2
66   Sedgly] F2 *; seagly MS, F1
10   I sweare a] MS; —— a F1-2

Her fathers hand set to it, and *Moroso's*:
I do not dream sure, let me read again,
The same still: tis a contract.
    Tra.   Tis so *Rowland*;
And by the vertue of the same, you pay me
An hundred pound to morrow.
    Row.   Art sure *Tranio*,   15
We are both alive now?
    Tra.   Wonder not, ye have lost.
    Row. If this be true, I grant it.
    Tra.   Tis most certaine,
There's a Ring for you to, you know it.
    Row.   Yes.
    Tra. When shall I have my money?
    Row.   Stay ye, stay ye,
When shall I marry her?
    Tra.   To night.
    Row.   Take heed now   20
You do not trifle me; if you doe,
You'l finde more payment, then your money comes to:
Come sweare; I know I am a man, and finde
I may deceive my selfe: Sweare faithfully,
Sweare me directly, am I *Rowland*?
    Tra.   Yes.   25
    Row. Am I awake?
    Tra.   Ye are.
    Row.   Am I in health?
    Tra. As far as I conceive.
    Row.   Was I with *Livia*?
    Tra. You were, and had this contract.
    Row.   And shall I enjoy her?
    Tra. Yes, if ye dare.
    Row.   Sweare to all these.
    Tra.   I will.
    Row. As thou art honest, as thou hast a conscience,   30
As that may wring thee if thou lyest; all these

28   this] MS, F2 *; his F1

To be no vision, but a truth, and serious.

Tra. Then by my honesty, and faith, and conscience;
All this is certaine.

Row.   Let's remove our places.
Sweare it again.

Tra.   I sweare tis true.   35

Row. I have lost then, and Heaven knows I am glad ont.
Let's goe, and tell me all, and tell me how,
For yet I am a Pagan in it.

Tra.   I have a Priest too,
And all shall come as even as two Testers.

                    Exeunt.

                Scaena Quarta.

        Enter Petronius, Sophocles, Moroso, and Petruchio
                born in a Coffin.

Petron. Set down the body, and one call her out.

            Enter Maria in blacke, and Jaques.

You are welcome to the last cast of your fortunes;
There lies your husband, there your loving husband,
There he that was *Petruchio*, too good for ye;
Your stubborn, and unworthy way has kild him   5
Ere he could reach the Sea; if ye can weep,
Now ye have cause begin, and after death
Do something yet to th'world, to thinke ye honest.
So many teares had sav'd him, shed in time;
And as they are (so a good mind goe with 'em)   10
Yet they may move compassion.

Mar.   Pray ye all heare me,
And judge me as I am, not as you covet,
For that would make me yet more miserable:
Tis true, I have cause to grieve, and mighty cause;

35   I sweare] MS; By —— F1-2
13   yet] MS, F2 *; ye F1

And truely and unfainedly I weep it.   15
   Soph. I see there's some good nature yet left in her.
   Mar. But what's the cause? mistake me not, not this man,
As he is dead, I weep for; Heaven defend it,
I never was so childish: but his life,
His poore unmanly wretched foolish life,   20
Is that my full eyes pity, there's my mourning.
   Petron. Dost thou not shame?
   Mar.   I do, and even to water,
To think what this man was, to think how simple,
How far below a man, how far from reason,
From common understanding, and all Gentry,   25
While he was living here he walkt amongst us.
He had a happy turn he dyed; ile tell ye,
These are the wants I weep for, not his person:
The memory of this man, had he liv'd
But two yeers longer, had begot more follies,   30
Then wealthy Autumne flyes: But let him rest,
He was a foole, and farewell he; not pitied,
I meane in way of life, or action
By any understanding man that's honest;
But onely in's posterity, which I   35
Out of the feare his ruines might out live him
In some bad issue, like a carefull woman,
Like one indeed born onely to preserve him,
Denyd him meanes to raise.

       Petruchio rises out of the coffin.

   Petru.   Unbutton me,
I vow I die indeed else? O *Maria*,   40
Oh my unhappinesse, my misery.
   Petron. Go to him whore; I sweare if he perish,
Ile see thee hang'd my selfe.
   Petru.   Why, why *Maria.*

---

39   S.D. *Petruchio rises out of the coffin.*] MS; *om.* F1-2
40   I vow I] MS; —— I F1-2
42   I sweare if] MS; —— if F1-2

Mar. I have done my worst, and have my end, forgive me;
From this houre make me what you please: I have tam'd ye,   45
And now am vowd your servant: Look not strangly,
Nor feare what I say to you. Dare you kisse me?
Thus I begin my new love.

    Petru.   Once againe?

    Mar. With all my heart.

    Petru.   Once again *Maria*!
O Gentlemen, I know not where I am.   50

    Soph. Get ye to bed then: there you'l quickly know sir.

    Petru. Never no more your old tricks?

    Mar.   Never sir.

    Petru. You shall not need, for as I have a faith
No cause shall give occasion.

    Mar.   As I am honest,
And as I am a maid yet, all my life   55
From this houre since, since ye make so free profession,
I dedicate in service to your pleasure.

    Soph. I marry, this goes roundly off.

    Petru.   Go *Jaques*,
Get all the best meat may be bought for money,
And let the hogsheds blood, I am born again: 60
Well little *England*, when I see a husband
Of any other Nation stern or jealous,
Ile wish him but a woman of thy breeding,
And if he have not butter to his bread,
Till his teeth bleed, ile never trust my travell.   65

    Enter Rowland, Livia, Byancha, and Tranio, as from mariage.

    Petru. What have we here?

    Row.   Another morris, sir.
That you must pipe too.

    Tra.   A poore married couple
Desire an offering sir.

    Bya.   Never frown at it,

64   his bread] MS *; thy bread F1
65   his teeth] MS *; thy teeth F1
65   S.D. *Tranio, as from mariage,*] MS; Tranio. F1 *

You cannot mend it now: there's your own hand;
And yours *Moroso*, to confirme the bargaine.   70

 Petron. My hand?
 Mor.   Or mine?
 Bya.   You'l finde it so.
 Petron.   A trick,
I sweare, a trick.
 Bya.   Yes sir, we trickt ye.
 Liv.   Father.
 Petro. Hast thou lyen with him? speake?
 Liv.   Yes truly sir.
 Petro. And hast thou done the deed boy?
 Row.   I have done sir,
That, that will serve the turne, I think.
 Petru.   A match then,   75
Ile be the maker up of this: *Moroso*,
There's now no remedy you see, be willing;
For be, or be not, he must have the wench.
 Mor. Since I am over-reach'd, let's in to dinner,
And if I can Ile drink't away.
 Tra.   That's wel said.   80
 Petro. Well sirha, you have playd a tricke, look to't,
And let me be a grandsire within's twelve moneth,
Or by this hand, Ile curtaile halfe your fortunes.
 Row. There shall not want my labour sir: your money;
Here's one has undertaken.
 Tra.   Well, Ile trust her,   85
And glad I have so good a pawn.
 Row.   Ile watch ye.
 Petru. Lets in, and drink of all hands, and be joviall:
I have my colt again, and now she carries;
And Gentlemen, whoever marries next,
Let him be sure he keep him to his Text.   90

Exeunt.

Finis.

72 I sweare,] MS; By —— F1-2

EPILOGUE

The Tamer's tam'd, but so, as nor the men
  Can finde one just cause to complaine of, when
They fitly do consider in their lives,
  They should not raign as Tyrants o'r their wives.
Nor can the women from this president   5
  Insult, or triumph: it being aptly meant,
To teach both Sexes due equality;
  And as they stand bound, to love mutually.
If this effect, arising from a cause
  Well layd, and grounded, may deserve applause,   10
We something more then hope, our honest ends
  Will keep the men, and women too, our friends.

COMMENTARY

I. EMENDATIONS OF ACCIDENTALS

The lemmata are those of the present text, and all seventeenth-century readings are provided. When the alteration differs from that of any seventeenth century source, no source is indicated.

I.i

2 Pudding's] F2; Puddings MS, F1
18 hue] MS, F2; huy F1
47 her,] MS; ∼. F1-2
48 pound] F2; pounds MS; ponnd F1
49 *Tra.*] MS, F2; *Tra*: F1
52 egges] MS; ∼, F1-2
70-71 Will ye ... Gentlemen.] Will ye walke? / They'l ... Gentlemen. F1-2; Will you walk? / They'l ... gentlemen, MS

I.ii

84 lungs] MS, F2; longs F1
134 desperate] MS, F2; disperate F1
159 still,] MS; ∼. F1-2
177 *Liv.*] MS, F2; ∼. F1
199 'Cheere wench] MS; ∼? F1-2
191 have,] MS, F2; ∼. F1
199 now, to visit you.] now to visit you. MS; now, / to visit you. F1-2
208 S.D. *Maria and Byanca*] MS; *om.* F1-2
220 way?] MS, F2; ∼. F1

I.iii

22 while.] ∼. MS; *om.* F1-2

34-38 *Petron.* Not a bed ... come.] ... rifle her, / ... in-tayl'd, / is yet? / ... cut it of, / ... come. MS; ... rifle / ... intayl'd / is it? / ... Ile cut / ... come. F1; ... rifle / ... intail'd, is / it? / ... I'll cut / ... come. F2

39-41 *Jaq.* Unless ... possible.] MS; ... like a / ... may untile / ... possible. F1; ... like a Daw, / ... the house, ... possible. F2

43 *rain,*] MS, F2; ∼. F1

43-48 *The wind* ... moneth.] ... back again, / ... truth is / ... cat-hole / ... victuall'd / ... this month. MS; ... *back again,* / ... the doores / ... murd'rer in it. / ... this moneth. F1-2

59 this? they are?] ∼?∼: MS; ∼.∼? F1; ∼?∼ – – F2

53-68 *Jaq.* Yes truly ... them.] ... desperate / ... stand vpon / ... composition; / ... cockt and / ... them. MS; ... too; and / ... ere yet / ... will not / ... as-sure you; / ... Bullets in / ... them. F1; ... too; and / ... yet bat- / ... give up / ... marching a / ... their mouths, / ... them F2

63-68 *Jaq.* Colonell ... yet.] ... Spinola's but a / ... but if / ... all yor / ... you shall / ... yet. MS; ... workes: / ... I am / ... venture a / ... mount / ... these / ... yet. F1; ... works: *Spi-* / ... am but / ... venture a / ... mount your / ... three / ... yet. F2

64 *Spinola's*] MS, F2; *Spinala's* F1

74-77 *Petru.* What are ... her.] ... Bedlam / ... hope, / ... noyse / ... her MS; ... Bedlam? / ... hope? / ... at Lon- / ... her. F1-2

82-90 *Soph.* Do, and be beaten ... charg'd sir.] ... I was / ... answer'd, / ... would haue / ... water worke / ... violence / ... quis nescit? / ... Ostend, / ... mounted / ... charg'd Sir. MS; ... I went / ... answered; / ... broke / ... flew from / ... duck'd / ... chamber's /

... Pewter / ... they / ... charg'd sir. F1; ... I went / ... knock'd / ... by force; / ... window with / ... Fryer, / ... *Ostend,* / ... quickly / ... charg'd sir. F2

92-94 *Soph.* And all ... go up.] MS; ... small / ... score / ... go up F1; ... shot, / ... hit / go up. F2

102-103 *Petru.* I know ... hundred;] ... Maiden-head / ... or two. / ... yes, / ... hundred; MS; ... your end, / ... Maiden-head / ... two. / ... hundred; F1-2

132-133 me from / A Chicken ... wiving?] me from ... hatching MS; me from ... hatching, / ... wiving? F1-2

219 Maudlin, / That's my] Maudlin, thats / my F1-2; Maudlin. / that's my MS

224 maids, they'l carry.] maydes, / they'l carry, MS; maids, they'l / carry. F1-2

232 the beauty] MS, F2; thy beauty F1 *

245 you] MS, F2; ~, F1

269-270 devill, / The downe right] diuell, the downe right MS; devill, the downe right F1; devil, the down- / right F2

271-277 Ile devill ... recreant.] ... the old / ... all my / ... you see / ... 'm & / ... recreant. MS; ... will: I'le / ... no pie. – – – / ... fine danc – – / ... recreamt. F1; ... bring / ... taken down / ... Gentlemen, / ... and by this / ... 'em out, / ... recreant. F2

281 *Mor.*] MS, F2; ~. F1

I.iv

7-8 *Ped.* You'l finde ... women – –] MS; ... Fiddle / ... women – – F1-2

11 reason;] MS; ~. F1; ~, F2

II.i

3 weight,] F2; waight, F1

51 horses.] F2; ~; F1

52 rumor?] F2; ~; F1

II.ii

12 S.D. *Maria*] MS, F2; ~. F1

 13 wench,] MS, F2; ∼. F1
 63 fellow,] MS, F2; ∼. F1
 83 doe 'em] MS, F2; doe th' em F1
112 This] MS, F2; Thls F1

II.iii

  1 doe] MS, F2; yoe F1
     man?] F2; ∼, F1; ∼. MS
 21 such] MS, F2; snch F1

II.iv

35-36 . . . destroy 'em, / . . . of 'em. / *Enter Pedro.*] . . .
       destroy 'em / . . . of 'em. Enter Pedro. MS; *Enter Pedro.*
       / . . . destroy 'em, / . . . of 'em. F1-2
   45 Parish,] MS; Parish. F1-2
   56 main] F1-2; manie MS
69-71 . . . Beares against the Cannons / of two church-
       wardens, made it good, and fought 'em / & in the
       churchyard after even song.] . . . beares against / the
       cannons of two church-wardens, made it good / and
       fought 'em & in the church yard after euen song. MS;
       . . . Beares against the Cannons / Of the Town, made
       it good, and fought 'em F1-2
88-89 Away then, / And] MS; Away then, and F1-2
   94 S.D. *Exeunt.*] MS, F2; *Exe* F1

II.v

  5 S.D. Exeunt.] ∼. MS, F1-2

II.vi

  8 Petru.] MS, F2; ∼: F1
 32 loose.] F1; ∼. MS, F1
42-43 Tyrants. . . . silence.] F2; Tyrants.– – –Song / . . . thou?
       / . . . in / . . . Lanskett. / . . . Harke. / . . . silence. MS;
       Tyrants. / . . . peep't in *Song!* / Lansket. / . . . Harke.
       / . . . silence. F1
   57 S.D. *Enter . . . Women.*] MS; *All the women above.* F1;

All the women above. Citizens and Countrey women.
F2

 61 No, believe me, I never] MS; No believe, / me I never
    F1-2
 64 Learnedly] MS, F2; Learuedly F1
117 *Enter Livia above. / Mor.* How, *Livia*?] MS, F2; Moro.
    How Liuia. Enter Liuia aboue. MS
120 't had] F2; t' had MS, F1
146 importun'd,] ~. MS ~. F1-2
152 you] F2; ye MS; yo F1
161 this inserted] MS, F2; this / inserted F1

III.i

 34 Why?] MS, F2; ~. F1
 46 him.] MS, F2; ~. F1
 62 *Tra.*] MS, F2; *Fra.* F1
 64 *Tra.*] MS, F2; *Fra.* F1
 84 leave] MS, F2; ~. F1

III.ii

  6 H'as] MS; Has F1, 'Has F2
21-22 whores / Had] MS, F2; whores had / F1
 26 somer salt] F2; Summer sett MS; sober salt F1
 27 fetch'd] F2; fetcht MS; fetchd F1
 42 o're] o're. MS; ore F1-2
 47 h'as] MS, F2; has F1

III.iii

  5 truly; do you] MS; truly; / Do you F1-2
 19 *Soph.*] MS, F2; ~, F1
 66 th'] MS, F2; 'th F1
 77 now?] MS; ~. F1-2
 79 rheums;] F2; rhumes, MS; hewms; F1
105 credit;] MS, F2; credit; F1
108 be.] MS, F2; ~. F1

III.iv

 11 young] MS, F2; youg F1

 17 *Row.*] MS, F2; *Rew.* F1
 48 young] MS, F2; yonng Fl *

III.v

22-23 Now daughter, / How dos my sonne?] How daughter,
       / how does my sonne, MS; Now daughter, how dos my
       sonne? F1-2
25-26 you gon, / If you mean to save your lives: the sickness.]
       ye gone / if you haue a care to saue your liues, the
       sickness, MS; you gon, if you . . . the sickness. F1-2
40-41 Masters: / Ho, you] masters; you MS; Masters: ho, you
       F1-2
42-43 me here: / Am I] MS; me here: am I F1-2
   49 me? first] MS; me? / First F1-2
   62 from] MS, F2; frow F1
  111 doubles,] MS, F2; dobles, F1

IV.i

   31 and] F2; add F1
  102 young] F2; youg F1

IV.iii

   15 *Enter Livia.* / By. Ho *Livia.*] F2; Bian. Ho Liuia! Enter
       Liuia MS; By. Ho, *Livia. Enter Livia.* F1

IV.iv

    8 S.D. *Servant.*] *Serv.* F1; Ser. F2; *occurs one line earlier
       in* MS
   39 *Tranio,*] MS, F2; Tranio' F1

IV.v

  7-8 for me, / And other] MS; for me, and other / F1-2
   70 *Soph.*] MS, F2; ∼. F1
   78 tatle.] MS, F2; tatle F1
  103 satiety,] MS, F2; saciety, F1
  133 *Petru.*] MS, F2; ∼. F1
  154 *Soph.*] MS, F2; *So h.* F1

188 *Mar.*] MS, F2; *Mir.* F1
200 hast] MS, F2; ha'st F1
201 thou] MS, F2; thouc F1
   Mar.] MS, F2; *Mir.* F1
212 Fare] MS, F2; Far F1
228 S.D. *Maria.*] MS, F2; ∼. F1

V.i

  4 seems] MS, F2; sems F1
 16 Has] MS, F2; Ha's F1
 22 How?] MS; How. F1-2
 31 byth' by] MS; by'th by F1-2
 59 be] MS, F2; by F1
 69 Pray] MS, F2; pray F1
76-78 I have abus'd . . . spit at him,] I haue abus'd this man perintiously; / Was neuer old man humbled so, / I haue scorned him and call'd him nasty names, / I haue spitt at him, MS; I have abus'd . . . man humbled so; / I have scornd . . . nasty names, / I have spit at him, F1-2
120-121 Come Gentlemen, / The showre] Come gentlemen, the showre MS, F1-2
146 There.] MS, F2; ∼ . . F1
203 journey's] MS, F2; journeys F1

V.ii

 60 *Jaq.*] MS, F2; ∼. F1

V.iii

 28 *Row.*] MS, F2; *Rew.* F1

V.iv

71-72 A trick, / I sweare,] A trick, I sweare, MS; A trick, / By —— F1-2
 82 twelve moneth,] twelue month MS; twelvemoneth F1-2

II. HISTORICAL COLLATION

Substantive and semi-substantive readings of all editions are collated; variants with their sigla appear after the square bracket. The lemmata are from the present text, and the omission of a siglum indicates that the source concerned agrees with the text.

Title Page

1-5] *om.* MS

Persons

  1 The Persons . . . Play.] F2, Waller; *om.* MS, F1; Dramatis Personae. 1711 *
  2 Men.] 1711, Sympson, Colman; *om.* MS, F1, F2, Weber, Dyce, Waller

3-22] F2; *om.* MS, F1

  3 *suitor to Livia.*] *om.* Dyce
  4 *Two Gentlemen, friends to Petruchio.*] his [Petruchio's] friends. Dyce
  7 *Gent.*] Gentlewoman 1711
    in love with *Livia.*] *om.* Dyce
 10 *witty*] *om.* Dyce
 14 Porters,] Porters, Servants. Dyce
 15 Women.] *om.* Weber, Dyce
 16 *A chaste witty Lady,*] wife to Petruchio, Dyce
 17 *Mistriss to Rowland.*] *om.* Dyce
 18 *and Commander in chief.*] *om.* Dyce
 19 City Wives,] City-women, Dyce
 20 Countrey Wives,] Country-women Dyce

To the relief . . . were drunk.] *Who come to the relief of the Ladies.* Sympson, Colman; *om.* Dyce
21 Maids.] Maids, and Waiting-Woman. Dyce

Prologue

1-20 *om.*] MS
10 *War,*] ∼. F2
13 *Expressions*;] ∼, F2

I.i

S.D. with Rosemary,] *om.* MS
God] Heauen MS
2 proof;] ∼, MS, F2
wench,] ∼. MS, F2
4 more?] ∼. MS
true: Certaine,] ∼, ∼, MS; ∼, ∼: Sympson, Colman
7 Dragon;] ∼, MS
12 her?] ∼. MS
16 *Mor.*] *Mar.* F2
17 stubbornes,] MS; sobernesse, F1, F2, 1711, Sympson, Colman, Weber, Waller; sourness, Mason, Dyce
20 she?] ∼, MS
22 maid?] ∼. MS
23 God . . . woman,] heauen had made me a woman, MS
24 be– – –] ∼. MS
29 wisdom, ∼. MS; ∼. F2
35 Breeches, out of feare] breeches out of feare, F2
36 yet.] ∼, MS
40 this] his MS
soule– –] soule, MS; soule– –, F2
46 Drink,] Sleep MS
48 these] this MS
weeks.] weeks F2
49 S.D. *with . . . Wine.*] om. MS
57 Lady day: O my] Lady day, a'my MS
58 Ring?] ∼, MS

59 a] at MS
63 ev'n] even F2
64 God] heauen MS
    S.D. *Jaq.*] *om.* MS
66 you'll] you'ld MS
68 now?] ∼, MS
69 both.] ∼? MS
71 wip't him now.] Impt him. MS; wip'd him now. F2

I.ii

1 Now] Nay MS
2 words‑ ‑ ‑] Sympson, Colman, Dyce; ∼. F1 *
6 You‑ ‑ ‑] ∼, MS
   way.] ‑? MS, Colman
7 Twill] 'Till Colman
   a] *om.* MS
8 his] this MS
9 love] loves MS
11 *Row.*] *Rom.* F2
20 h'as] has MS, Colman, Dyce
23 Cracus,] Croacus: F2, 1711; Crocus, MS, Sympson,
    Colman, Weber
29 what a faith] MS, Sympson, Dyce; what faith F1 *
31 Laid] MS, F2, 1711, Waller; Lasd F1; Lac'd Sympson,
    Colman, Dyce; Laced Weber
33 makst] makest MS
42 Yfaith] Indeed MS
    rather‑ ‑ ‑] ∼ MS
47 you? Goe] you, MS
48 *Enter . . . Maria.* / . . . conscience] . . . conscience /
    Enter . . . Maria. MS
57 you] ye MS
63 But . . . him‑ ‑] *om.* MS
64 to 't?] to it? MS
65 Twill] 'Till Colman
    stranger] MS, Sympson; stronger F1 *
66 I am perfect,] Ile doe it. MS

67 have I] I have F2, 1711; I've Sympson

68 Leap'd into this gulf of marriage, and Ile do it.] Leapt in this gulf of marriage MS

69 poorer] poore MS

miracle. Now cosen,] miracle vpon him MS

70 *Following this line MS inserts lines 75-79: Bya.* This is . . . example.

78 fears] *'fears' in MS altered from 'feare' in darker ink.*

81-84 *MS arranges lines:* . . . Wench,

. . . reuels

. . . a corke,

. . . sport-start'd.

81 of heart is't,] o' the hart is't MS; of heart is't? F2

82 Revels] MS *; Rebels F1

up rowse] rowse up F2

84 sport-starv'd?] sport-start'd MS

84-85 Deere sister, / Where] Deare sister where MS

85-86 Why at Church, wench; / Where I . . . thus: I . . . now.] Why? at church where I . . . thus, / I . . . now. MS

87-88 You are an asse; / When . . . once, thy modesty / Will . . . Pins.] Y'are an asse, when . . . once / thy modesty will . . . pins. MS

90 *Livia?*] ∼. MS

91 mad.] ∼? MS, Colman, Weber, Dyce

91-92 . . . so must you be, / . . . acquaintance; marke me *Livia.*]

. . . so must you be, marke me Liuia, / . . . acquaintance, MS

93 Tis bed time.] *om.* MS

95-96 Thine . . . My] thy offerings to protract, and to keep f / fasting my MS

101 there are] there be MS

Comets] *written over some now indiscernible word in* MS

102 there's] there is MS

106 Tis as easie with] 'tis with MS

111 mothers] womans MS

118 ev'ry] euery MS
121 pleasures are] pleasure is MS
129 disobedience] MS, Colman, Weber, Dyce; obedience F1-2, 1711, Sympson, Waller
130 Which ... imputation,] (which ... imputation) MS
147 *Mar.*] *om.* MS
148 these] those MS
149 halla,] hallow, MS, F2
151 that hath] that has MS
152 an hundred] a hundred MS
153-154 ev'ry ... ev'ry] euery ... euery MS
156 foundred] founder'd MS
158 down] downs' MS
160 tired] tir'd MS
164 all] *om.* MS
175 wanting] wonting F2
180 Then] There Dyce, Mason
    ye] you MS
186 as you] as ye MS
187 followed.] follow'd MS
189 *Mar.*] *om.* MS
190-194 *Bya.* 'Cheer ... say.] Mari. How Bianca. / Bian cheere wench. / Mari. those wits ... say. MS
190 You.] Yee, MS
201 *Mar.*] *Jaq.* 1711
202 *Jaq.*] *Jap.* 1711
204 y'ar] you are MS
206 you'l] you will MS
211 heads together] heads; MS
212 them] 'em MS
216 this] these MS
    weddings?] wedding Mason
    a] *om.* MS
217 trick,] ranck, MS

I.iii

Designation *scena tertia.*] *om.* MS

S.D. *and Sophocles.*] Sophocles. MS
 1 home] have MS, F2 *
 2 nights] night MS
 4 next? als? MS
 7 your trot] you troth MS
    Gallants.] gallant. MS
 8 stuffe] MS, Sympson *conj.* ; staffe F1 *
10-11 *Tra.* A good ... thy prayers.] *om.* MS
 12 us. Will ... sonne?] us, well son, well MS
 18 at] ac F2
 27 man.] men.' Dyce
 30 miscarried so;] Mason, Weber, Dyce; miscarried so,
    MS; miscarried; So F1 *
 33 and] or MS
 34 o' me] a me, MS
 35 it?] yet? MS
 37 off:] of, MS
 45 *And you*] ye MS
 47 murd'rer] murder MS
 48 not thou] thou not MS
 52 fellow?] ~. MS
 55 ere] are MS
 56 will not) wont Sympson
 62 Heavens] loues MS
 65 but a poore] a poore MS
    you'l] you'l'd MS
 66 Ile] sir, Ile MS
 68 enter it] enter in't MS
 69 *Jaques.*] ~, MS
 71 sir?] ~. MS
 72 cool'd] cold. MS
 74 mad?] ~, MS
    Bedlam?] ~. MS
 75 hope?] ~: MS
 76 fearfull,] fearefully, MS
 78 she tongue?] she this Tongue? Sympson
 79 wedding-night?] ~, MS

83 th' doore,] the doore MS

85 window] windore MS

89 window] windore MS

93 tongues] tongs MS

94 ye dare] you deare MS

95 window] windore MS

97 what intrenc'd?] Intrencht MS; what, are you intrenc'd? Sympson

99 why who] Why, pray who Sympson

104 twenty,] twenty Sir, MS

106 this present houre,] this houre MS

107 never will] will never MS

111 cry you . . . you] crie ye . . . ye MS

112 do's] doth MS

114 (I . . . night)] I . . . night. MS

115 So as't follows.] so as'tfol wols F2

118 seale] seals MS

120 Bugs-words] Bug-words. F2, 1711, Sympson, Colman

121 heare sir,] heare her Sir, MS
     God] heauen MS

122 sir.] *om.* MS

123 bestowd] bestowed MS

126 jesting] ∼? MS

131 charge when] charge us when Sympson

132 Heaven blesse] MS, Colman, Weber; Blesse F1; Bless F2, 1711, Dyce, Waller; Heav'n bless Sympson

133 is this wiving?] *om.* MS

135 me?] ∼. MS

136 forc'd] forced MS

142 nor . . . nor] or . . . or MS

146 'em,] them, MS

149 except] accept F2, 1711; *altered from what was perhaps 'accept' in MS*

153 i'ld] I would MS, Weber; I'll F2, 1711, Sympson, Colman, Waller; I'd Dyce

156 ev'r] e're MS

161 sir, that] Sir, / that MS

163 die lowsie, if] dye lowsie / If MS
    knavery to stock] knauery, / To stock MS
165 you, . . . you] ye, . . . 'ye MS
166-167 It is so: / And till] It is so, and till MS
173 a woman that can feare] a woman / that feare MS
176 for you,] for ye, MS
189 monstrous:] monstruous MS
    the] *written over some now indiscernable word in* MS
191 thee, . . . thee– – –] thee . . . thee, MS; thee, . . . thee,
    whore; Colman, Weber
192 th'] the MS
196 on't.] out. MS
208 remedy?] ~. MS
209 Cudgell.] ~, MS
210 in?] ~, MS
211-212 Rebels, next / *Tyrone*,] rebels next Tyrone MS
213 beare you,] beare ye, MS
218 me?] me now? Sympson
223 You.] ye. MS
224 girthes. you'l] girths, / you'l MS
234 mind's] minds MS
235 maskes] markes MS
238 And] *om.* MS
242 too] for MS
244 then alayes,] then like alayes MS
250 hand-well:] ~, ~, MS; ~, ~; F2
    I shall] shall I Sympson
    yet?] ~. MS
251 wither'd] withered MS
    Jewry,] Jury, F2
253 soon?] ~, MS
257 sitting] setting
261 you know,] ye know MS
262-268 There my cause lies . . . Centinels.] there lyes my
    cause, . . . famous / . . . breaker, / . . . off, / . . . you,
    nay looke so bigg, / . . . thinke yee? / . . . Sentinels. MS
267 night to all,] Night all, Sympson

268 ye dare] you dare MS

269 ev'n] euen MS

273 Death taken] MS; – – –taken F1-2, 1711, Sympson, Colman, Waller; Pox, taken Dyce, Weber

278 but those] but these MS

283 each provide his tackle,] each / prouide him to his tackle MS

287 jaded?] ∼. MS

S.D. *Exe. Omnes.*] Exeunt. MS

I.iv.

Designation *Scaena quarta.*] om. MS

S.D. *Enter Rowland, and Pedro, . . . doores.*] Enter Rowland at one doore, Pedro hastly at the other. MS

2-3 pardon me, / I am] pardon me I am MS

4 hasty– – –] ∼. MS

Pedro?] ∼. MS

5 married?] ∼. MS

6 *Row.* Why?] MS *shows 'Rowl.' written over 'Ped.'*

9 *Iaques?*] ∼. MS

10 businesse?] ∼. MS

16 yon] you MS, F2

Fare ye well] fare you well MS

17 my] thy MS

18 S.D. *Iaques.*] om. MS

Enter Sophocles. / Custards, . . . Fiddles,] Custards . . . fidles / Enter Sopho. MS

20-21 *Rowland.* / I cannot stay to] Rowland, I cannot stay / to MS

32 Never] Neu'r MS

34 armies] MS, Weber, Dyce, Colman; Armes F1; Arms F2, 1711, Sympson, Waller

35 Mistresse?] ∼. MS

39 Farewell. . . . Farewell] fare you well. . . . Fare you well MS

40 in't,] ∼? MS

41 stay ye;] stay, MS

41-44 Enter . . . Gold, / . . . him / . . . comes,] That . . . gold
/ . . . him Enter Liuis and / . . . comes. Moroso as
vnseen by hir MS
48-49 looke sir / Without] looke, Sir, without MS
   50 Twenty Spur-Royals] I thank thee MS; Twenty spur-
ryals Colman, Weber
   56 Excellent] Gramercy for that MS
   57 knockle] MS; knuckle F1-2; noddle Mason
   63 women] woman MS
   65 breakes] breake MS
   67 provide you,] prouide for you, MS
   70 She's mine from all the world:] *om.* MS
S.D. *gives him a box o'th eare and Ex.*] She gives Moroso a box a'th eare, & Exit. MS
   71 How's this? I do . . . save you.] Is't come to this, / Saue
you. MS
   72 thee– – –] you MS
S.D. Wrings him by th' nose.] *om.* MS
   73 thank me] thuck me MS
S.D. *Exit.*] MS, Dyce; *om.* F1-2
   74 of ye,] of you MS

II.i

1-59] MS *omits this entire scene.*
    4 and no] and is no F2
   19 within's] within these Weber
him] him. F2
   21 it?] it; F2
   27 within's] within these Weber
   31 Moneth] month F2

II.ii

Designation Scaena Secunda.] Actvs II^{us} Scaena j^{ma} MS
S.D. alone.] F2; *om.* MS; $\sim$. F1
    1 but get in] gett in but MS
    4 finde] finds MS
    5 Do not beleeve] beleeue not MS

.7 y'on] yo'nd MS

12 *Qui va la*?] MS, Colman, Weber, Dyce; *Cheval'a* F1-2
    Che va la? *Sympson*

15 you come] ye come MS

16 I come] ∼∼ – –MS

29 Sinon] Simon 1711

49 us, and to your selfe.] vs and to our cause. MS

58 off] *om.* MS
    Fillyes:] Flies; Sympson, Colman, Weber, Dyce

60 Bilbo blade,] bilboe blade, MS; *Bilboa* blade F2

61 most] *om.* F2, 1711

62 Coughes,] Coughs. F2

68 Has] hath MS
    you sweare this,] and truly ye sweare this truly MS

74 Nev'r feare] Nere feare MS

81 An] a MS
    yeare] years F2

83 customs.] customs, F2

84 you] ye MS

88 bee'st] beest F2

89 fail] fall MS

96 nor legges,] no legs MS

97 i'th] a'th MS

98 Thou'lt be] th' root be MS

105 (like . . . furies)] like . . . furies, MS

108 office,] offence! Dyce; *suggested* Heath

109 (Though . . . now)] though . . . now, MS
     hither,] first MS

119 You . . . you,] ye . . . you MS

121 our Offrings.] our offerings. MS; our Off'rings. F2; your
     offerings. Dyce

II.iii

S.D. *and Tranio . . . doores.*] at one doore, Tranio at
y^e. other. MS

1 *Rowland*?] Rowland, MS

2 look'st ill:] lookest ill? MS

can] *om.* MS

3 knew] kew MS

7 choak'd] choaked MS

9 a Schoole question] a great schole question MS

15 could] cood' MS

17 he] be F2

21 rack] Wreck Colman, Weber, Dyce

23 Why] *om.* MS

27 be?] ∼. MS

28 *Row.*] *Raw.* F2

32 or] *om.* MS

33 I doe beseech] I beseech F2

Following this line MS *inserts line 36*: Our . . . friendship, *and leaves blank space enough for six lines.*

36 Our . . . friendship,] *om.* MS

39 her . . . her:] here . . . her, MS

43 first] *om.* MS

enjoy] ioy MS

II.iv

S.D. *Moroso, and Sophocles.*] Sophocles Moroso MS

5 by– – –] by this hand MS; by Heaven, Dyce

12 comes] come MS, F2

17 *Nell a Greece,*] Nell of Greece, MS

19 these] those MS

21 (Believe . . . should)] beleeue . . . should; MS

24 For] and MS

25 surer] sooner MS

26 amendment.] mendment. MS

27 hangd] hang'd MS; hang'd MS

31 with– – – –] ∼, MS

32 moneths] months, MS, F2

37 devils] euils MS

43 pray silence.] pray you silence. MS

51 and] aad F2

57 tossing] toasting Colman

60 Codsheads,] Godheads F2, 1711, Sympson

64 and] or MS
65 zeale,] zeals, MS
67 o'th] a'th MS
68 *Soph.* Lo . . . impatience.] MS *places this line after*
    Jaques speech line 78: Drunk hard . . . victor.
    you] ye MS
72 Another,] Anothe F2
79-85 *Ped.* Then are . . . war for.] *om.* MS
84 Britaine] Briton Weber, Dyce
87 you must] ye must MS
90 o'th] a'th MS
92 doe; but] doe, / but MS

II.v.

1-5 Enter three·mayds, . . . Tis sufficient.] Enter 3 Country
     wenches at seuerall doores.
     I.   How goes your busines girles?
     II.   A foot and faire
     III. If fortune fauer vs, away to your strengths
           we are discouer'd else.
     I.   The country forces are arriu'd, begon.
     II.   Arme and be valliant, thinke of our cause.
     III. Our Iustice I: I: I: 'tis sufficient. MS; *om.* F2,
           1711, Sympson, Colman, Weber, Waller

II.vi

Designation Scaena Sexta. Colman, Weber, Dyce,
Waller; *om.* MS; Scena tertia. F1-2, 1711; SCENE IV.
Sympson
S.D. *and Tranio.*] Tranio. MS
3   resolv'd] resolued MS
7   that's] there's MS
8   Why] They MS
    do?] ~, MS
9   I with] I, with F2
14 which] (~MS
    Don Hercules] Dom Hercules MS

15 Sicely,] Cicely? F2
   have] hade MS *altered from* 'haue'
20 done?] ∼ – – – MS
22 ev'n] euen MS
26 you] ye MS
30 flownder with] fownder with MS
32 . . . the world. / *Tra.* and loose / *Music above.*] . . . the
   world. Musique aboue. / Tranio & loose MS
33 on my] a my MS
34 God] long MS; Heaven F2, 1711, Sympson, Dyce
   Jaques?] ∼. MS
36 it] ∼, F2; ∼. MS
38 (They] (that MS
   S.D. *SONG.*] *In* MS *under the word* 'Song.' *a spot of
   sealing wax–containing paper fibers apparently not from
   the opposite page–indicates that perhaps a song was at
   one time attached here.*
62 drunk] drank F2, 1711, Sympson, Colman, Weber,
   Waller
63 are– – –] ∼. MS
68-69 woman, / A comely,] woman, Comly MS
75 these?] this? MS
   shall] sall MS
78 into] in MS
79 you good] MS *shows* 'good *you* good' *with the first*
   'good' *crossed out.*
80 Catechiser] cathe chiser MS
83 come] came MS
88 we'l] weel'e MS
89 and then all] and eu'n all. MS; and all F2
95 hood] *added in* MS *by a caret and in another hand.*
96 I] I'll F2
99 main Bottles,] manie bottels MS
104 recreant,] MS, Dyce, Mason; recant, F1 *; MS *shows*
   'recant' *crossed out and* 'recreant' *added in another
   hand.*
106 chambring:] chambering, MS

112 Crests,] creastes, MS
     Plackets,] MS, 1711, Colman, Sympson, Waller;
     Plackets. F1-2; *plackets* Weber, Dyce
115 wars:] warres MS
117 She's] shee is MS
118 Heare] Heard MS
119 ye,] you MS
129 There's] There is MS
131 Apothecaries.] th' apothecary's. Sympson, Colman
132 It] I Mason, Weber
     sir.] *om.* MS
134-135 *Liv.* He will undoe me . . . make him lustie.] *om.* MS,
     F2
136 S.D. *Reads.*] *om.* MS
143 pound] pounds MS
147 monstrous.] monstruous. MS
152 you] ye MS; yo F1
153 you fore] ye fore MS
156 No, Ile take that oath; / But have] No, Ile take that
     oath, but haue MS
     you] ye MS
157 you do] ye doe MS
158 these Articles] this creed MS
160 honesty– – –] honestie MS
162 command] commanded F2
169 you] ye MS
170 Ne'r] Neuer MS
172 *Petru.*] *Petro.* F2

III.i

1   you] ye MS
    S.D. *Enter Tranio, and Rowland.*] Enter Rowland &
    Tranio. MS
9   *misereri's,*] Colman, Weber, Dyce; Mistrisses, MS, F2,
    1711, Sympson; miseries F1, Waller
15 dance. I] dance; I'le MS
21 tis] *om.* MS

23 hartely] hartly, MS heartily, F2
26 gilt, calfe,] calf with the white face, MS
29 *Tra.*] *Tro.* F2
30 more man.] more a man. MS
32 at best] at the best MS
40 Ye . . . if] you . . . (if MS
41 (Which] which MS
42 gibbrish;] gibberish, MS
44 Raigne] raignes MS
46 You] your MS, Dyce
    licks] licks *altered from "like" in* MS
47 A] O MS
    pox] MS, Colman, Weber, Dyce; – – – F1-2, 1711,
Sympson, Waller
60 again?] ∼. MS
62 women?] woman. MS
67 pound] pounds MS
69 and my] an my MS
77 you as] ye as MS
    she now hates you.] she now hates ye. MS; now she
hates you. F2
80 an . . . if you] a . . . if ye
81 Have you] Haue ye MS
    No, no sir.] No more Sir. MS
83 for th'bell;] forth-bell, MS
85 you,] ye, MS
86 how] what MS
    pound] pounds MS
87 you.] yee. MS
89 Shal't] 'Shalt MS
90 the] yᵒʳ MS

III. ii

Designation *Scaena Secunda.*] om. MS
5 O' my] A my MS
7 him?] ∼, MS
9 he kiss'd her,] she kist him, MS

12　prayers] Payers F2
20　those Amorities,] these Amorites MS
22　hallowed] hallow'd MS
　　div'lish] develish MS
23　*Jaq.*] *Jac.* F2
　　didst thou] didst' MS
24　Cavaliero?] Cauelero? MS
30　the] *om.* MS
31　ballasse.] ballast– – – Colman, Weber
33　it– –] ∼. MS
41　tippled] tippl'd MS
43　*Cinque-a-pace*] MS, F2; Cinque-pace F1
46　see] saw Dyce
　　master] Master– – – F2

III.iii

Designation *Scena tertia.*] *om.* MS, Weber, Dyce
1　S.D. *Enter Petruchio, and Sophocles.*] Enter. Petruchio
　　Sophocles. MS night?] night. MS
2　courage?] ∼. MS
5　you] *om.* MS
7　I past] I had past MS
9　*Petru.*] Petro MS
11　washt] wash MS
13　could,] coo^{r}d MS
15　appetite– – –] appetite? MS
17　Refus'd] refused MS
19　to her,] vnto her, MS
21　on the] of the MS
23　pain] pains F2
　　for . . . nettl'd] (for . . . netled) MS
26　started?] startled MS
27　answered] answer'd MS
29　Butler] botler MS
32　nights] monthes MS
36　Stay ye, stay ye,] Stay, stay, MS
38　keenely] kindly MS

41 spoke's] spoke is MS
45 verjuce,] verjuice, F2
49 *Maria . . . and woman. / . . .* live a Doxy.] . . . a doxy Maria at y^e. doore & Seruants. MS
52 ev'ry] euery MS
54 pearle.] pearles MS
55 those] these MS
   hangings] hanings. F2
60 cuts] cutte MS
65 suit] suite MS
74-75 doer, / Did] doer, did MS
80 tild] til'd MS
82 thy] your MS
84 built] build MS
86 for young Scolds.] for yor young scoldes. MS
91 gilt;] guilt, MS
94 and justice] *om.* MS
101 weigh'd,] way'd MS
103 duty?] duty. 1 MS
114 sweet] good MS
126 duty.] duty. 1 MS
127 friends] friend MS
137 never] neu'r MS
143 it, rots take me.] MS; its – – – F1, 1711, Sympson; it's – – – F2, Waller, Colman, Weber, Dyce; it. Mason
145 wintering] wyntring MS
146 These] this MS

III.iv

Designation Scaena Quarta.] *om.* MS; SCENE III. Weber, Dyce
1 S.D. *Tranio, and Rowland.*] Rowland, Tranio. MS
7-8 you, / At Plays, and Cherry-gardens.] you at plays / & cherie gardens. MS
10 him] *om.* MS
12 out a] out of a Sympson
13 poore] pure MS

15 woman.] man. MS

17 hansome.] handome. MS

24 you lov'd me – – –] ye loued me, MS
   deerly;] dearely, MS

25 lov'd] loued MS

28 you . . . you] ye . . . ye MS

34 mine] my MS

36 o'] a' MS
   makes] gets MS

40 you,] ye, MS

42 much– –] much. MS

43 you;] ye,

46 farewel. . . . Farewel.] farewell. – – – . . . farewell, Sir MS

48 H'as] 'Has MS

50 He's] 'Is

52 Lady: wipe] lady to wipe MS

55 *Moroso*] Moroso– – – MS

III.v

Designation Scaena quinta.] *om.* MS; SCENE IV.
Weber, Dyce

 1 S.D. *Jaques and Pedro.*] Pedro & Jaques. MS

12 th'] ye MS

18 ye,] you MS
   is he] is a MS

20-21 fellow: / No man that has been] Fellow: no man that
   has / Been MS S.D. *Sophocles, and Petronius*] Sophocles; Petronius, Liuia, Bianca & Tranio. MS

23 you] ye MS
   Now] How MS
   S.D. *Enter . . . Tranio.*] om. MS

25 you gon,] ye gone MS

28-29 My husband has it now; / Alas he is infected, and raves
   extreamly:] my husband has it now, amd raues ex-
   tremely. MS

30 me] *om.* MS

33 Hath sent a watch by this time;] has sent a watch, I

thank 'em, MS

34-35 long is't / Since it first tooke him? / ... three houres.
/ *Enter Watch.*] long is't since it first took him – –
Enter yᵉ Watchmen. / ... 3 houres, MS

36 wits: – –O here's] wits, my freinds, MS

37 friends,] fast MS

40 S.D. *Petruchio within.*] *om.* MS
Petru.] Petruchwᵗʰ in. MS

41 ho,] *om.* MS

45 goodman] goddman MS

51 Ev'ry] euery MS

55-64 If any man misdoubt me ... of your Velvet costard.]
om. MS

65 Death, gentlemen,] MS; – – – – –Gentlemen F1-2, 1711,
Sympson, Waller; Pox, gentlemen, Colman, Weber,
Dyce

66 ye] you MS

70 And the ... pay for't] *Following this line* MS *adds*:
Petro. fetch a Doctor presently, and if he can doe no
good on him, he must to Bedlam.

70 S.D.-72 *Exit Doctor* ... but one way.] *om.* MS

73 you] ye MS

74 save our selves sir. / He's past all worldly cure.] saue
our selves, hee's past all / worldly cure. MS

78 friends– –] freinds. MS

80 who's] who F1-2, Waller

81 you] ye MS

82-83 you, the good ... care you] ye, the ... care / ye MS

92 instant – – –] instant, MS

95 Do you] Doe ye MS

96 am wel, as] am as well as MS

97 2] 1. MS
you were] ye were, MS

98 if you] if ye MS
lives,] lifes MS

100 I sweare Ile] MS; – – – –Ile F1-2, 1711, Sympson,
Waller; By heav'n, Colman; By heaven Weber, Dyce

101 1] 2. MS
102 he's dangerous,] *om.* MS
103 2] 1. MS
     devill] De'l Sympson; de de'il Colman
     hinmost,] hindmost, 1711, Sympson, Colman, Weber
     S.D. *Exit watch*] Exeunt MS
104 shoot;] shot MS
105 ye] *om.* MS
116 Quartern-ague,] quartane ague, MS
118 H'as] has MS; He'as F2
119 he] a MS *added with a caret and in a different hand*
124 again:] MS, Colman, Weber, Dyce; again: I could rail
     twenty daies; F1 *
131 too] two F2
132 suffer'd,] sufferd MS
137 those] these MS

IV.i

1-107 *om.* MS
   12 should] would F2
   20 Give] Give me Sympson
   61 sweep] sweet Sympson, Colman
   70 then, then Boyes then,] then, boys, then Sympson, Col-
       man, Weber
  107 too;] doe; Sympson, Colman

IV.ii

Designation *Scaena Secunda.*] Weber, Dyce; Actus IIII.
Scaena j^{ma} MS; *om.* F1-2 *
   2 ev'n] euen MS
   7 (Better . . . over)] better . . . ouer MS
      these] those MS, F2
   9 Ev'n those] Euen these MS
  11 S.D. *Exit Ped. and Iaq.*] Exeunt Iaques and Pedro. MS
  20 Not certaine . . . had I, / *Enter Maria.* / And] Enter
      not certaine . . . had I? – –Enter Maria. / Maria & MS
  23 the fault is] this fault MS

29 ordain'd] ordained MS
30 and two old] and the two old MS
32 h'as a] 'has 'a MS
37 Alas win] alas would win MS; *'would' added with a caret and 'win' corrected from some other word—both in a different hand in* MS
38 make] made MS
41 (though . . . foolish,)] though . . . foolish MS
42 Lov'd him, Oh . . . for't!] loued him (o . . . for't) MS
46 came] come MS
47 a] *om.* MS
53 not come] not to come MS
56 to be] *om.* MS
58 dealing,] meaning, MS
59 wether,] *'away' has been crossed out and 'wether' written above it in a different hand in* MS
62 thanke me one day] one day thanke me Weber
    for: alas,] for, MS
63 watch'd] watch MS
65 to] *om.* MS
66 Heav'n blesse me.] Heauen blesse me, MS
69 you are] ye are MS
70 At least, . . . you . . . so,] (at least . . . ye . . . so) MS
76 breach] breacth MS; *altered from 'breath' with a caret and in a different hand in* MS
77 you kick] ye kick MS
78 vow'd] vowed MS
82 ly'd] lyed MS
83 O'the Shire?] a' t'h sheire MS
87 (Because] because MS, F2
88 temper)] temper, MS
92 away] *om.* MS
96 you'l] youl' MS
97 ever you] euer ye MS
98 What you] What ye MS
99 families] family Sympson, Dyce
101 But ever . . . sir.] *om.* MS

113 veng'ance,] vengeance, MS
116 you,] ye MS
121 continuing] continue MS
127 thou thing] thoug thing MS
129 wither'd,] witherd MS
137 may well] may MS
139 do'st] doos't MS
142-143 defie you. / And my last] defie you, and my last MS
147 till] tell MS
     I doe] doe I MS
149 but] a MS
153 would] wolld MS
156 S.D. *Mar.] om.* MS
158 Fayries] furies, MS
159 made.] a man MS

IV.iii

Designation *Scaena Tertia.] om.* MS; *Scaena Secunda*
F1 *; SCENE III. Weber, Dyce
1 Mistresse, you] Mrs / you MS
2 ready I told you of?] readie / I told ye? MS
3 ready but to] readie, / but to MS
4 an Asse, you must] an asse, / you must MS
   constru'd,] conster'd MS
5 peirc'd] perced MS
6 find little] find a little MS
8 pound] pounds MS, F2
11 you] ye MS
15 S.D. *Exit Tra.]* Exit MS
17 Carrick.] Carrack. F2
21 minc'd] mixed MS
23 fear'st] fearest MS
24 Even] Ene MS
   Gallowes] galiowes MS
26 not.] not. F2
38 nev'r] ne're MS
39 o'th] a'th MS

42 these?] this? MS

43 you] ye MS

44 That which] that that which MS

47 pray be] pray ye be MS

48 you:] ye MS

  Doe] So. MS

51 honesty,] honestly, MS, 1711, Sympson

  S.D. *Exeunt.*] *Exunt* F2

IV.iv

Designation *Scaena Quarta.*] *om.* MS; Scaena Tertia.
F1 *

1 on my] a my MS

2 you,] ye, MS

3 you.] ye, MS

4 You] Yee MS

5 your] yor *added with a caret in* MS

6 you] ye MS

7 avoid 'em feare:] auoid them. MS; avoid 'em. F2

  No, on my word sir] No I protest Sir Enter seruant.
  MS; '*Seruant*' *altered from* '*Seruants*' *in* MS

8 you.] ye. MS

  S.D. *Servant.*] *Serv.* F1; *occurs one line earlier* in MS

10-12 *Row.* Why your Master? . . . What of her?]

                  Row. Why your Master,

                  Seru. My pretty M^isLiuia,

                  Row. What of her?

                  Serv. O S^r his jewell

                  Row. With the gilded button MS

13-14 o'th . . . o'th . . . O'th] a'th . . . a'th . . . A'th MS

14 very sick:] and very sicke, MS

16 fare you well] fare ye well MS

18 S.D. *Exit*] *Ex.* F2

  . . . see him. / . . . bottle. / *Exit Servant.*] . . . see him.
  Exit Seruant . . . bottle, MS

24 old] od MS

25 daintily,] daintly MS

26   to'th] to the
27   by you.] by ye, MS
37   you– – –] ye MS
40   forty] fourthy MS
44   you.] ye. MS; you– – – F2
47   Which] wth MS
48   Jack o' Lent] jack a lent MS
49   Compters:] counters, MS
50   bargaine;] bargaine MS
55   then, . . . dar'st] then,– – . . . darest, MS

IV.v

Designation *Scaena Quinta.*] Weber, Dyce; *om.* MS;
Scaena quarta F1 *
1 S.D. *and Pedro.*] Pedro. MS
  5   Plough again, and] Plough, and F2, 1711, Waller
  6   numberd:] numbred, MS
16-17   alas sir / What a] alas Sir, what a MS
18   thinkes] think's MS
22   do's] does MS
24   give the neighbours] giue neighbours MS
      Larme,] larum MS
29   read of] read yet of MS, Sympson
30   know'st] knowest MS
35   S.D. *Enter Ped.*] Enter's Pedro MS
36   Weaves] waues MS
      wickednesse:] wickednes.– – MS
39   Ev'n] easie MS
      not teach] not to teach MS
40   men have their] man hath his MS
42   do's] does MS
43   She's] Shee is MS
44   if't] if it MS
46   (Saving . . . reverence)] Sauing . . . reuerence MS
      i'th cut] i'th' cut F2
49   any speake] any one speak Sympson
52   *Sophocles,*] Sophocles. Enter Sophocles MS

52-53 what / Did] what did MS
   54 sirha,] *om.* MS
   55 S.D. *Enter Sophocles.*] *occurs in line 52 in* MS
   57 she is] shee's MS
      Sir, I] I MS
   59 rid] ride MS
   60 Pray, be] Pray, Sir, be Sympson
      not mistaken:] not you mistaken, MS
      hand] light MS
   61 wife's as] wife is MS
   63 deceiv'd] deceiv'ed MS
   64 Beleeve me,] I sweare MS
   69 you] ye MS
      S.D. *Enter Maria.* / And pray continue so.] And pray
      continue so. / *Enter* Maria. F2
   76 a case] case MS
   81 understanding)] vnderstanding MS
   82 you] ye, MS
   83 sweeter– – – –] sweeter. MS
      An] A MS
   86 Nev'r] Neuer MS
   87 have day] have a day MS
   88 I speake] Ile speake,– – MS
   90 you're well] y'ar' well MS
 105 She's] She is MS
 108 woman-hood,] man-hood MS
      morall] mortal F2
 110 and know] and I know MS
 123 ordan'd] ordained MS
 125 imploy'd] imployed MS
 126 (That] that MS
 127 you christian)] ye a Christian, MS
 129 you,] ye, MS
 130 you,] ye, MS
 131 see you] see ye MS
      to you,] to ye, MS
 132 forget] forgiue MS

141 you:] ye; MS
142 (And . . . me)] and . . . me, MS
143 weakly] weakely MS
     you,] yee MS
145 you:] ye, MS
     you,] ye, MS
155 through unknown Seas plough] plough through unknown
     Seas Sympson Seas] sea MS
164 you] ye MS
165 Do'st] Doe'st MS
170 Signour,] senior MS; Signior, F2
175 i'th day,] in the daye, MS
178-180 That, that must . . . offer'd me, and strongly,] to haue
     temptations, and no little ones / daily and hourely
     offer'd me, and strongly; / that, that must make me
     spoken of hereafter, MS
180 offer'd] offered F2
182 you.] ye. MS
183 my troth,] MS; my soul, Colman, Weber, Dyce; my– – –
     F1 *
184 not you] you not MS
     no,] om. MS
185 try her,] MS, Dyce; try, sir F1 *
186 for] om. MS
189 that] those MS
194 Cataya,] Catayna F2
195 climes] climats MS
196 o'th] of the MS
197 you] ye MS
200 me o'th] me out a'th MS
203 wouldst] would MS
     hangd] hanged F2
207 other of my] others a' my MS
     Nev'r] Ne're MS
208 You] ye MS
213 you] ye MS
218 For] (for MS

219 els,] else MS

222 you want Limon-waters,] ye want lemmon water MS

226 custody – – –] custody MS

228 S.D. *Maria.*] *om.* MS

235 fayths] faithes MS

V.i

1 S.D. *with foure papers.*] *om.* MS

2 discern sir.] discerne it Sir. MS

5 spoke] spake MS *altered from 'spoke'*

14 that] *om.* MS

17 O] Oh, F2

26-27 carriage. . . . *En. Rowland and Tranio.*] carriage Enter
Rowland & Tranio . . . MS

27 *Petron.* Now] Now MS
Get] Will MS
other too.] other two. MS

28 Good ev'n] Goodd e'n MS
you are] y'are MS
too,] *added with a caret in* MS

31 unto her] into her MS

35-38 Yes sir.] . . . Well sir. *om.* MS

39 'twere] it MS

43 have] had MS
o'th] oth' MS

45 your] you MS

46 execution.] executions. MS

47 till] tell MS

49 never was] was neuer MS

52 kind of farwell of you,] kind farewell of ye, MS

53 wandring] wandering MS

58 her, you shall] her shall MS, F2

60 So be] Why soe be MS

62-64 What ere she saies . . . teatish.] What ere she sayes, you
must beare manly, / for her sickness has made her
somewhat peeuish MS; What ere she saies . . . pettish F2

67 Daintely] daintly MS

an hundred] a hundred MS

68 S.D. *Enter Livia discovered abed, and Moroso by her.*]
Enter Liuia. sick carryed in a chaire by seruants; Moroso by her. MS; Livia *brought in on a bed,* Moroso *by her.* Weber; *Curtains are drawn by* PETRONIUS, *and* LIVIA *is discovered in bed,* MOROSO *standing beside her.* Dyce; S.D. *occurs one line earlier in* MS

69 Pray draw 'em] Pray beare her MS

71 O very sick,] O sick, MS

71-72 somewhat / Better] somewhat better MS

72 I . . . lightsommer,] *om.* MS

76 perniciously;] pertiniously; MS

80 dos:] does, MS

82 (Oh God my . . . fellow:] *om.* MS; (Oh my . . . fellow: F2

85 living:] extant; MS
purging-comfits] comfits MS

90 Ev'n] euen MS
this reverent] MS, F2 *; his revernt F1, Colman, Weber

95 Jumbled] I- //// umbled MS

102 you;] ye, MS

115 you] ye, MS

116 then:] *altered from a now indiscernible word in* MS

116-117 Pray stay . . . peruse 'em,] Pray stay then giue me the papers, / and lett me peruse them, MS

120 ye] you MS

124 you] your MS

127 cry'd] cryed MS

129 this?] it is MS

133 lie] sitt MS
your] our MS

135 Now if] and if MS
power] pow're MS

136 heare] haue MS
S.D. Rowland, Tranio, Moroso.] Moroso, Rowland, Tranio. MS

137 lamentations: pray] lamentations, / pray MS

144 heartily he weeps!] hartly he weepes. MS
Pen] the Pen MS
145 Ev'n] euen MS
156 draw . . . close,] *om.* MS
162 fare ye well;] fare well, MS

V.ii

Designation *Scaena secunda.*] *om.* MS
1 S.D. Enter . . . Hampers.] Enter Iaques & Pedro; and
Porters with a trunke and hampers. MS
3 He'l] heel' MS
8 soule,] word MS
10 'em] them MS
11 God] Heauen MS
12 ye:] thee MS
13 ye,] you, MS
16 powerfull] carefull MS
18 spar'd] spared MS
19 presently.] instantly. MS
O' that] A that MS
26 amongst the Whitings,] among the whiting MS
29 o'shore] a shore MS
34 meet] met Dyce
angred,] angerd'
35 her tongue, her tongue.] her tongue! MS
38 lickrish – –] lickerish, MS
39 other] more MS
47 of her– – –] Colman, Weber, Dyce; of her. MS; of – – –
her F1-2, 1711, Sympson, Waller
48 Get ye in,] gett you in MS
53 Even] eu'n MS
56 S.D. *Exit Soph.*] Exit. MS
61-62 And he, / That man,] And he, that man MS
62 Heav'n] heauen MS
63 ev'n] en'e MS
fadings.] MS; longings. F1 *; Fadding F2, Sympson,
Waller

67 spurd, with] spurd, / with MS
  S.D. *Exeunt.*] *om.* MS

V.iii

Designation *Scena tertia.*] *om.* MS
 1 S.D. *and Tranio*] Tranio MS
 8 ye.] ye, – – MS
 9 on't:] A on't – – MS
10 I sweare a] MS; – – – – – – a F1-2, 1711, Waller; By
   heaven a, Sympson, Colman, Weber, Dyce
11 Moroso's:] Morosoes, MS
12 again,] againe – – MS
15 An hundred] a hundred MS
16 ye] you MS
19 Stay ye, stay ye,] Stay, stay, MS
21 trifle me;] trifle with me MS, Dyce
26 Ye are.] you are, MS
29 if ye] if you MS
   these.] this, MS
31 may] nay F2
   lyest; all these] ly'st all theis MS
35 I sweare] MS; By – – – – F1-2, 1711, Sympson, Waller;
   By Heaven, Colman, Weber, Dyce

V.iv

Designation *Scaena Quarta.*] *om.* MS
 1 S.D. *and Petruchio born in a Coffin.*] Petruchio in a
   Coffin, carried by Seruants. MS
 2 S.D. *and Jaques.*] Jaques, Pedro. MS; Jaques *and* Pedro.
   Dyce
 6 ye can] you can MS
 7 ye have] you haue MS
   after death] after's Death Sympson
11 ye all] you all MS
14 and] a MS
39 Denyd] denyed MS
   S.D. *Petruchio rises out of the coffin.*] MS; *om.* F1-2,

1711, Sympson, Colman, Waller; *Rising* Weber, Dyce

40 I vow I] MS; – – – – F1-2, 1711, Sympson, Waller; Oh, God, Colman; By Heaven, Weber, Dyce

42 I sweare if] MS; – – – – if F1-2, 1711, Sympson, Waller; By Heaven, Colman, Weber, Dyce

49 heart.] heart, sir. MS

51 ye] you MS

56 houre since, since ye] hour, since you MS; hour, since ye F2

65 S.D. *and*] *om.* MS

71-72 A trick, / I sweare,] A trick, I sweare, MS; A trick, / By – – – F1-2, 1711, Sympson, Waller; A trick, / By Heaven, Colman, Weber, Dyce

74 have done sir,] have, Sir, F2

75 *Petru.*] Petro MS

78 For] *M*or. F2

81 you] ye MS

82 moneth,] month MS

Finis.] *om.* MS, F1-2

EPILOGUE

1-12 EPILOGUE. . . . friends.] *om.* MS

III. CRITICAL NOTES

The *Oxford English Dictionary* serves as the source for all definitions found within the critical notes unless a given note is specifically documented to another source.

I.

1-20 PROLOGUE. . . .] F1 places the prologue just before the epilogue at the end of the play. MS begins with the text and thus has neither title page, dramatis personae, nor prologue. MS also omits the epilogue at the end of the play where there is ample space for the scribe to have copied it if it had been accessible to him. It is likely that the prologue and epilogue were inaccessible to him or had not yet been written and that neither is by Fletcher. Internal evidence in the prologue, as Dyce points out, indicates that it was added for some revival of the play; the epilogue was most likely written at the same time.

1 S.D. *Rosemary*]. Weber: "This herb was not exclusively used on mournfull occasions; but, being supposed to strengthen the memory, was also carried at weddings. The supposed signification of it may be more fully deduced from the following stanza of an old song, printed in the last edition of Evans's Ballads, and entitled "A Nosegaie alwaies sweet, for Lovers to send for Tokens of Love at New yeres Tide," &c.

> Rosemarie is for remembrance
> Between us day and night,

> Wishing that I might always have
> You present in my sight.

In Randolph's Milkmaid's Epithalamium (poems, 4th ed., 1652, 12, p. 102) a young girl wishing for marriage sings,

> Love quickly send the time may be
> When I shall deale my rosemary!

1 God] MS reads "Heauen"; MS frequently has this variant for "God". See note I.ii. 42.

4 Tis too true: Certain,] The punctuation seems correct as it stands in F1-2. Loosely paraphrased it reads, "I agree with you. I certainly think that her father has dealt harshly with her . . ." Sympson and Colman feel that the folio punctuation confuses the sense; their interpretation is, "It is certainly too true. I think that her father . . ." The pointing of MS allows either interpretation.

17 stubbornes] MS "stubbornes" is certainly correct; it might easily have been misread as "sobernesse" and it accords perfectly with the demands of Catherine's character. Mason suggests "sourness" on the grounds that it more accurately approaches the temperament of Catherine than the folio reading of "sobernesse"; Dyce adopts his suggestion.

25 I would learn to eat Coales with an angry Cat] "This seems to allude to some inhuman trick played with cats" (Weber). The line seems to be no more than figurative – angry cats hiss as if they have coals in their mouths.

26 Prevent] Anticipate.

27 ramping] Storm or rage with violent gestures.

34 Colstaves] "A stick for the purpose of carrying a burden between two people. It was a familiar household requisite, and a ready weapon. A rough form of popular punishment (inflicted especially on a husband who allowed himself to be beaten or abused by his wife) was

to be set astride a pole and be carried in derision about
the streets."

38   *Babylon*] Tranio is probably referring to the old ballad
Babylon in which an outlaw kills two of three sisters
before the third identifies him as their brother, Baby
Lon.

39   And by my troth] So MS; F1-2 "And on my word" is
milder and would be more acceptable to those, such as
Herbert, who objected to oaths.

41-42   His very frowne, if she but say her prayers /
Louder then men talk treason, makes him tindar;]
Sympson suggests: "*Her very* Sound, or, as it might be
wrote nearer to the trace of the Letters in *Chaucer's*
Manner, Her very *sown, i.e.* Voice, and then the passage wou'd be Sense."
Mason offers: "The very sound, if she but say her
prayers, etc."
Weber comments: ". . . But all these emendations are
so far from the trace of the letters that none of them
bid fair to have been the original reading. Nor do we
see the slightest reason for any emendation; the original
text affording a meaning perfectly explicit and clear,
and in entire conformity with the whole of the context,
and the uniform character of Petruchio: "If she but
says her prayers louder than men speak treason, he puts
on such a frown as makes him appear, or, by the or-
dinary process of inordinate self-indulgence, actually
makes him become, inflammable like tinder."
Heath and Dyce agree with Weber, and MS supports
F1-2.

43   Diall] A clock or watch.

44   water-worke] A system of machinery for raising, con-
veying or distributing water; in 1594-5 a water-work
was erected near Queenhithe to serve the middle and
west parts of the city. Dyce adds, ". . . the noise of
which is considerable".

46   Drink, . . . pisse] It can readily be seen that MS "pisse"

comes under the heading of what Herbert called "obsceanes" and was bowdlerized in the F1 text to "unready".

Just why "Drink" in F1 is "Sleep" in MS escapes any
satisfactory explanation.

52-53 This old sport must have egges, ... with Muskadell]
Egges were considered an aphrodisiac, and from the
context one can deduce that muscadel wine must have
been considered to have a similar property.

54 broods his Master] Nourishes or cherishes him.

56 neat] Pure or undiluted.

58 run at Ring] Dyce paraphrased Weber's note to read:
"A quibbling allusion to the sport called Running at
the Ring, when the tilter, riding at full speed, endea-
voured to thrust the point of his lance through, and to
bear away, the ring, which was suspended at a fixed
height."

The obvious sexual implications of Jaques' speech are
but a small sample of the many remarks the doting,
old Moroso endures.

62-63 This single thrummin of a Fiddle / Without a Bow,]
Jaques is making fun of old Moroso by referring to his
obvious impotence, while the other side of this double-
entendre suggests Livia's desire to marry Moroso.

66 steale] To effect or accomplish clandestinely or un-
perceived.

69 One charge had serv'd for both] I.e., Moroso could
have a double wedding with Petruchio.

71 wip't him now.] MS reads, "Impt him now." The scribe
misread his copy-text, for the meaning is that Sophocles
has got the better of Moroso or has wiped him.

I.ii

Designation *Scaena Secunda*] This is the only scene
division indicated in MS.

2 If your affections be not made of words– – –] The pointing of this clause is unusual; the terminal mark of

punctuation should be a dash since the speech is inter-
rupted by Livia. Sympson alters the punctuation to a
dash, and Colman and Dyce follow his example.

4 Is there none neere us?] A parenthetical question.

6 Why then take this way.] Colman points this sentence
with a question mark. Mason (and subsequently Dyce)
say, "The point of interrogation destroys the meaning; he
is not asking a question, but pressing Livia to follow
his advice."

23 counterfeit Cods,] Weber in recalling Chaucer's use of
the word *cod* feels that there might be some indelicate
meaning in this passage; however, Dyce offers a more
sensible definition: spurious or adulterate civet-bags.
Cracus] A kind of tobacco.

29 what a faith] So MS; Sympson, in his desire to regular-
ize the meter independently adopts this reading; Dyce
follows his example and calls attention to II, iii, 189:
"Whether that woman ever had a faith".

31 Laid out upon a Petticote] The independent agreement
of MS and F2 on "Laid" is significant. Sympson adopts
F1 "Lasd"; Colman, Weber, and Dyce chose to agree
with Sympson. The meaning is clear: Moroso's money
can kiss her behind and these kisses will be laid out
upon a petticoat.

35 Riders] A gold coin, having a figure of a horseman on
the obverse, formerly current in Flanders and Holland.

37 make use of me] To employ or maintain for sexual
purposes.

41 puling] Crying as a child, whining.

42 yfaith] MS "indeed", indicates that MS's source under-
went some censorship independent of that of the source
of F1. Herbert's records show that he censored the
play 21 October 1633; on 9 January 1633/4, Herbert
was instructed by the king to "take *faith, death, slight,*
for asservations and no oaths." The fact that the king's
order came after Herbert had censored the play is born
out by the number of times F1 has some milder form.

There are a few instances, however, where a milder form occurs in MS.

52 I had rather feel it.] F1-2 omission of this suggestive line suggests censorship. Its restoration from MS completes the preceding half-line.

60-61 Believe me, since his first wife set him going, / Nothing can bind his rage,]. Weber: "It is perhaps, not too bold a hypothesis to suppose, that Fletcher, being called upon by the ladies to revenge their cause upon Petruchio, and to transplant the laurels of victory from his head to that of a second wife, ... increased the value of the compliment intended for his countrywomen, by removing the residence of Petruchio from Italy to England, and giving the honour of having tamed the boastful Italian to an English virgin."

63 But if you suffer him—–] The scribe of MS inadvertently omitted this line, and a few lines later confused his text by misplacing lines 75-79 after line 70. Line 70 in MS reads: "Till I have wrought . . ."; after completing this line, the scribe lost his place and in picking it up again, found line 75: "Till I have run . . ." After copying the next two speeches, he realized his error and copied down the four-and-a-half lines he had omitted. There is a possibility that F1 may here be in error, but the metrics and sense of the passage argue against such a hypothesis.

65 and the stranger in you] So MS. From the context of the passage, Sympson independently proposed "stranger" for F1-2 "stronger". Subsequent editors neglected to to follow his example.

67 Curtius] *Oxford Companion:* "Lacus Curtius: according to legend a chasm appeared in the Roman forum in 362 B.C., which the soothsayers declared could only be filled if Rome's greatest treasure were thrown into it. Whereupon Marcus Curtius, saying that Rome could have no greater treasure than arms and valour, mounted his steed in full armour and leapt into the chasm, which

thereupon closed over him."

78 made] MS "mayds", possibly the correct reading.

fears] In MS this word has been altered from 'feare' in a darker ink, most likely by the same person who made numerous additions and corrections to the manuscript in a secretary hand, which Professor Bald describes as: "undoubtedly seventeenth-century".

82 *Paphos* Revels] This refers to the revelries (specifically the sexual indulgences) of Paphos, a city of Cyprus sacred to Aphrodite.

83 a Cork:] ". . . the dry, withered body of Moroso" (Dyce).

83-84 tell / The clock] To count the hours as shown by the clock; hence to pass one's time idly.

84 o'th lungs] By the use of the lungs; i.e., in exercise or heavy breathing.

sport-starv'd] MS "sport-start'd" is obviously a misreading by the scribe.

95 keepe fasting] The scribe of MS intended to end this line with "fasting" but changed his mind after writing the first letter and began a new line with the word. This would seem to indicate that the scribe was trying faithfully to reproduce the lines of the text exactly as they appeared in his copy-text. It seems unlikely that he proofread his copy after the lines had been written since he does not correct the line.

100 Devest] Undress.

101 Comets] The scribe of MS wrote a wrong word and then altered it to "Comets".

107 *Lucina*] Goddess of light and childbirth.

117 Joynture] A sole estate limited to the wife, to take effect upon the death of her husband.

129 Besides the disobedience of a wife,] So MS; obedience F1-2; Colman suggested: "We read, DIS*obedience*, which *Maria's answer* certainly confirms. Again, *obedience*, or, as Seward would read, DUE *obedience*, is no *heavy imputation*, but DIS*obedience* is; and supplies the syllable required by Seward to complete the

measure, and, what is of more consequence, agrees with the sense of the context."

146 *Bya.* That's a good wench] This half-line, found only in MS, adds very little, but the metrical problems of the lines without it argue for its inclusion in the text. In the lines which follow this, MS omits the speech prefix, "*Mar.*", and thus gives the lines to Byanca. This is most probably an error since the tone of the speech is very much in keeping with Maria's attitude, and in the very next speech Livia refers to the speaker as "sister". Maria and Livia refer to each other as sisters, and Byanca refers to them as cousins.

148 Eyasses] Young hawks from the nest, or ones incompletely trained.

149 Lure] An apparatus used by falconers to recall their hawks, being a bunch of feathers attached to a cord, within which, during its training, the hawk finds its food.

150 Kites] Members of the falcon family and particularly voracious scavengers; the reputation of the kite was such that the term, kite, was applied figuratively to a sharper or rogue.
Haggard] A hawk caught after having assumed the adult plumage; hence, wild, untamed.

152 checks] False stoops, when a hawk forsakes her quarry for baser game.

155 quarry] The bird flown at by a hawk.
pitch] The height to which a falcon, etc., soars before swooping down on its prey.

156 foundred] To founder is to stumble violently, collapse, fall lame, or become struck fast in mire.

157 fling out traines] To throw out pieces of meat in a row to lead game to a desired spot.

180 Then Ile leave ye Ladies] Colman suggested that "Probably we should read, THERE, *I'll leave ye.*" Mason agreed that "there" is a better reading; Dyce, however, is the only editor to have incorporated the

change in text. The context and MS both argue against
the change.

188-194   *By.*   Good night: we'l trouble you no further.

     Mar.   If you intend no good, pray doe no harm.

     Liv.   None, but pray for you.

                  Exit Livia.

     Bya.   'Cheere wench.

     Mar.   Now Byancha,

     Those wits . . . all men say.]

The scribe of MS omitted the speech-prefix to line 189
and thus incorporated it into Byancha's speech, line
188. In addition he transposed the speeches of Byanca
and Maria in line 190; this transposition made it necessary for him to add the speech-prefix, "Mari". to
line 191 so that the speech would be attributed to the
correct speaker. The text is repeated here for comparison:

     By.   Good night, weel' trouble you no further,

         If you intend no good, pray doe no harm,

     Liv.   None but pray for yee,   Exit Liuia

     Mari.   How Bianca,

     Bian.   Cheere wench.

     Mari.   Those wits . . . say.

192   My rest is up wench, and I pull for that] Mason is
probably correct in suggesting that "my rest is up means
my stake is laid"; "pull for" thus means "draw [a card]
for". Weber did not favor the allusion to betting at
cards and argued that this passage had reference to
pulling the trigger of a musket which had to be steadied
on a rest. Whatever the allusion, the meaning is clear:
"Maria has made up her mind and is now ready for
action."

I.iii

5   lusty *Laurence*,]. Weber: "This probably refers to a tale
still common among the vulgar of the powers of a friar
so called. The alliteration was a powerful incitement

to the popularity of the phrase."

8 where's the stuffe boy, ha?] So MS; "staff" F1-2. Moroso is the constant butt of the bawdy jokes and in-
nuendoes of the younger men. The reference (in line 9)
to the empty hourglass completes the metaphor for MS
reading, "stuffe", and points once again to Moroso's
impotence.

Sympson conjectured that "stuff" rather than "staff"
is the correct reading here: "Tho' I take no Pleasure in
the raking into a Dunghil, yet the amending of Pas-
sages to the Honour of our Authors good sense, whether
innocent or obscene, is the Duty of every careful Editor;
for *Staff*, therefore, I propose reading *Stuff* and the following line seems to confirm the Alteration."

Ironically, he did not alter his text to agree with his
contention.

10 A good tough traine would break thee all to pieces]
An indelicate reference to Moroso's age and impotence
– a train being a tail.

18 *St. George* at Kingston,] Dyce gives the following note:
"I find, says Nares (citing the present passage, *Gloss.*
in V. *George, St,*), an allusion to a slanderous sign at
Kingston, on which St. George was represented as on
foot, and flying from the attack of the dragon's tail.
This was a most disgraceful representation of the favorite saint, and, till we have it further explained, we
cannot but wonder that it should have been tolerated."

21-22 *Soph.* His warlike launce /
Bent like crosse bow lath, alas the while]
These lines found only in MS were obviously cut for
obscenity. Their restoration to the text restores the
lineation.

24-25 *Tran.* That anie priuie S.ᵗ euen S.ᵗ Davy
May lash him with a leeke.]
Saint David, d. 588 (?) the patron saint of Wales, was
the first abbot of Menevia. He was known for his strict
rule and zealous missionary endeavors. Pilgrimages to

his shrine were frequent in the Middle Ages. These lines, found only in MS, were perhaps censored from the printed text because of a possible bawdy allusion in the word, "priuie".

26-27 Fly, fly, quoth then the fearfull dwarf; / Here is no place for living man.]
This is the reading of all early texts. Dyce, however, points out that this is a quotation from Spenser's *Faerie Queene*, B.1.C.1.st.13, and that "living man" should read "living men".

28 *Petru*. Well my masters, ...] As verse in MS, but beginning with this speech and continuing through most of the long speeches in the remainder of Act I, F1-2 set the lines in what appears to be prose; Sympson, Seward, and Theobald (the first editors) recognized the underlying verse structure and set the lines as blank verse. However, their insistence on perfecting the lines metrically led them to take unwarranted liberties with the text; subsequent editors also tried to correct the text, and as a result, line lengths vary markedly in all the editions. This editions follows MS except where a textual correction has made a change necessary.

30 miscarried so;] MS supports Mason's conjecture that the sense of the passage is probably clearer if the pointing is placed after "so" rather than after the verb as in F1-2. Weber and Dyce adopt Mason's reading.

35 coyle] Noisy disturbance, fuss, ado.

43-45 The wind and the rain . . . be lodged there] Weber: "This quotation from a ballad, seemingly very popular, occurs again in The Knight of the Burning Pestle, act iii, sc. 5 where it begins, 'Go from my window, my love, go.' It is quoted, also, in the Soldier's Fortune by Otway. Turned into a spiritual hymn, it occurs in the Scottish collection of Godly and Spiritual Songs, &c. 1621."

47 murd'rer] A small cannon or mortar used to clear the decks when an enemy boards a ship.

58 Bullets in their mouthes] "Before the invention of

cartridges, bullets were frequently carried in this manner . . ." (Weber).

64 Spinola] As Colman points out, this is Ambrosio Spinola, marques de Espinola (1569-1630). He was a Spanish general, born in Italy of a noble Genoese family, and fought in the Netherlands, capturing Ostend from Maurice of Nassau in a seige that lasted from July 5, 1601, to September 8, 1604.

Ditcher] One who makes and repairs ditches; Weber suggests that "ditcher" here stands for "pioneer"; that is, one of a group of foot soldiers who went ahead of the troops and dug the trenches.

there's a halfe-moon] Referring to the women's quarters, he means that they are fortified by a half-moon embattlement or are in a half-moon formation.

70 Beat back again] Driven back again by force.

88 a meere Ostend] Ostend resisted the siege of the Spaniards from 1601-04 and surrendered only after it was reduced to ruins and had reportedly cost the Spaniards 40,000 lives. Sophocles refers to this siege as being "meere" in comparison to the resistance that the women are prepared to present. Oliphant, *The Plays of Beaumont and Fletcher*, holds that this topical allusion gives evidence of a composition for the play of not later than 1604, "since it seems to imply that the famous siege is still in progress". See, however, Introduction, p.   .

89 pewter cannons] Chamber pots.

91 tantara] Imitative of the sound blown on a trumpet or sometimes of a drum.

93-94 Fire-locks, that at twelve score blanke / Hit to the heart:] Weber: "That is which will hit the mark, though the blank, (or white mark at which aim is taken) were twelvescore feet distance."

120 Bugs-words] In Welsh, bwg is a goblin or a ghost, and bug's words would be terrifying.

132 Heaven blesse me] So MS. F1-2 reads " 'Blesse me";

the apostrophe in "'Blesse" and the metrics of the line
indicate that MS is correct. Sympson, Colman, and
Weber independently insert "Heaven".

145 conditions] Qualities; disposition.

146 owes] Owns.

148 parcels] Parts; particulars.

154 Groats] A groat was a coin worth four pence.

155-156 the ablest / That ev'r leap'd out of Lancashire,] Weber:
"The Lancashire men are still celebrated for their
strength and dexterity at the sport of single-stick, being
frequently matched against the Somerset youths."
The alliteration of the phrase probably gave it more
popularity than the truth of its content, and "ablest"
seems to have obscene connotations in the context.

157-158 stand prating / Out of the window like a broken Miller!]
Here "broken" probably means bankrupt; Weber says
that millers commonly looked out of their windows
when they had nothing to do.

178 Low-bel.] Weber: "A sheep's or goat's bell in a forest.
This seems to be the present signification of the word;
Bianca, to whom the word is addressed, being the
rallying-point, the commander or bell-weather of the
rebellious ladies. It may, however, refer to another
signification of the term, *viz.* 'a kind of fowling,' as Dr.
Johnson explains it, 'in which the birds are wakened by
a bell, and lured by a flame into a net'." So *O.E.D.*

190 blessing that St. Dunstan gave the Devil] Dunstan was
Archbishop of Canterbury 960-988; he is generally re-
garded as one of the greatest Anglo-Saxon Saints. The
story referred to is that the devil tried to tempt Dunstan
by appearing before him in the form of a woman,
whereupon Dunstan siezed the apparition by the nose
with a pair of red-hot smith's tongs.
gave the Devil] "The" in this line is written over some
now illegible word in MS. See note, line I.ii.2.

191 I would give thee– – –] So F1-2; MS "I would give thee",
and the context indicate that a break in thought is in-

tended here. Colman and Weber read "I would give thee whore". Dyce correctly points out that 'whore' would have hardly been a word objectionable to the censors as the texts of Colman and Weber seem to indicate.

193 Rubarb] A medicinal root which is used as a purgative and astringent.

198 Jade] A sorry worn-out horse.

212 *Tyrone*] Hugh O'Neill, 2nd Earl of Tyrone, a very powerful chief in Ulster who sought aid from Spain in the Catholic revolt against England (1595-1601).

223 livery] Allowance of food to servants.

271 ten bones] "Ten fingers" (Weber).

280 perdue] Placed as an outpost, scout, etc., in a hazardous position; (lying) in ambush, in wait.

I.iv

6 *Row*. Why] MS shows "Rowl." written over "Ped". See note I.ii.2.

14 Sowse] Food preserved by pickling.

16 yon Rebels] Despite the agreement of F2 and MS in reading, "you rebels", the context of this passage quite clearly indicates that F1 is correct. Jaques is referring to the rebel women, not Rowland.

31-32 such a Regiment of Rutters / Never defied men braver:] Mason: "Rutters was a name given to a body of German troops in the service of France; but a play upon the word is here intended. Braver means here more bravely."

34 armies in the ayre,] So MS. Symphson and Theobald first suggested reading "Armies" for F1-2 "Armes"; however, Symphson did not make the correction in the text of their edition. Weber called attention to a similar reference in *Wit Without Money*: "– – – – fiery battles Seen in the air at Aspurge." All editors since Symphson have corrected their texts.

50 Spur-Royals] Gold coins of the value of fifteen shillings, chiefly coined in the reign of James I; so called from

having on their reverse the form of the sun with rays, resembling a spur-rowel.

57 knockle] So MS; F1-2 have the variant spelling "knuckle". There is most likely a bawdy allusion to the male sex organs here. The term knocking to suggest the sex act is recorded in a collection of old bawdy songs, *Pills to Purge Melancholy*, and in this frame of reference MS reading of "knockle" is probably correct. Mason suggested that the correct reading should be "noddle" since knuckles are not usually covered with hair. Weber points out that Rowland is being accused of his extreme youth and thus is not likely to be bald; the explanation, according to Weber, is that Livia means his chin when she speaks of his hairless knuckle.

61 ten-pound waste-coate] From the context it can be deduced that Livia merely regards a ten-pound waistcoat as an expensive garment. Weber has a long note in which he points out that strumpets were associated with such apparel; however the context does not warrant such a reading here.

II.i

4 Has sude his liverie] In feudal tenure, the court of wards took possession of a tenant's lands upon his decease. His heir, upon reaching maturity, could then sue out his livery and thus regain possession of the lands.

6 fumbling] Sexually impotent.

7 forehand] The position in front or above.
baffel'd] Disgraced.

12 Bastard] Any sweetened wine, but specifically a sweet Spanish wine resembling muscadel.

15 Hobby-horse] A fool or buffoon.

16 childe *Rowland*] Child was often used to designate a youth of gentle birth, a sir or knight. Shakespeare cites a ballad entitled Childe Rowland in *Lear* III.iv.187.

27 within's] Within these; Mason calls this a vile contraction which ought not to be continued.

34 toyes] Trifles or nonsense.

37 hansell] To use for the first time.

39 joynture] A sole estate limited to the wife, to take effect upon the death of her husband for her own life at least. In the succeeding lines Moroso makes a pun on the word.

43 demurrers] A pleading which, admitting the facts as stated in the opponent's pleading, denies that he is legally entitled to relief, and thus stops the action until this point be determined.

rejoynders] The defendant's answers to the plaintiff's replication.

45 crying ripe] I.e., Petruchio is crying that he is ready for action.

55 Draw] Micturate.

56 Cuck stooles] Chairs formerly in use for scolds, disorderly women, fradulent tradespeople, etc. in which the offender was fastened and exposed to the jeers of the bystanders, or conveyed to a pond or river and ducked.

II.ii

4 Sisters safety] "Sister's place of safety, her strong hold" (Mason).

7 Foxcase] Livia is referring to Moroso as a fox-skin.

9 Myrmidons] One of the warlike races of men from Thessaly who followed Achilles to the siege of Troy; hence faithful followers or friends.

19 kept up tame] Reared in a gentle manner.

27 hand-fast] Firm hold or grip with the hands. Here the word is used figuratively to mean their position or stronghold.

29 *Sinon*] The name of the Greek who induced the Trojans to bring the wooden horse into Troy. See Virgil's *Æneid*, Book II.

37 *Amazons*] A race of strong, female warriors alleged to
exist in Scythia.

44 That kill'd the Prince of *Orenge*] Colman and subsequent editors quote Reed: "This was Balthazar Ge-
rard, who murdered the prince of Orange at Delft, on
the 10th of July, 1584. The horrible punishments inflicted on this miserable wretch are thus related by a
writer who lived not very distant from the time in which
the transaction happened: 'Here first he had his right-
hand with a hot yron seared and cut off, which did the
deede, and cast into the fire: Next of all, with firie hot
pincers he had his flesh torne and pluckt off from sixe
parts of his bodie, which were most fleshie, *viz*. of his
breast, armes, legs, and buttocks, and those cast into
the fire; and his body, beginning from the lower part,
was with an axe chopt in peeces, his belly was ripped,
his heart was pluckt out and cast at the villaine's face
(yet in some life) and afterwards his head, being chopt
off, was with other foure parts of his bodie, as arms
and feete, set upon foure poles on foure turrits or ports
of the citie, fastened upon a long pole set upon the
turrit of the schoolhouse, on the back-side of the
prince's lodging; and whatsoever he had in his lifetime
about him was taken from him and given away.' A true
Discourse Historicall of the succeeding Governors in
the Netherlands, and the Civil Warres there begun in
the yeere 1565, &c. 4to 1602." (*B.L.*, p. 51.)

52 dride Jack] A dried fish; dried hake.

54 brokery] A broker's wares; anything second-hand or
stale.
doggs-ditch] I.e., Hound's Ditch a section of London
(Dyce).

58 Fillyes] The agreement of MS, F1, and F2 is decisive
for the present reading, and it is well known among
horsemen that colts will eat off the tails of the mature
horses with which they are pastured. Sympson, however, silently altered the text to read "Flies", and sub-

sequent editors have followed his example.

60 Bilbo] A sword noted for the temper of its blade.

62 fewterer] A keeper of grey-hounds, and thus an attendant.

A dry nurse] A person who has charge of young children.

63 a rob'd thing] I.e., a thing robbed.

65 One cast away on course beef] I.e., one who has to spend her life with a vulgar old man.

born to brush that everlasting Cassock] A cassock is a long coat; the implication is that Moroso would make a servant out of his wife, but the overtones of this whole speech by Byancha are bawdy.

67-68 as the Northeast passage / Has consum'd Saylors:] The Northeast passage was a passage for vessels along the northern coasts of Europe and Asia and was formerly thought of as a possible course by which to make voyages to the East. These northern routes were particularly windswept and turbulent. See Introduction, p. 19.

78 recreant] Unfaithful.

98 night-mare] A female monster supposed to settle upon people and animals in their sleep producing a feeling of suffocation.

99 say her Prayers back-ward] Weber: "This was supposed to be one of the most powerful spells of witch-craft. So in the last act, scene II., Petruchio says,
'If there be any witchcrafts, herbs, or potions,
Saying my prayers backward, fiends or fairies,
That can again unlove me, I am made'."

105 Keys] I.e., the keys to their cupboards, etc.

106 distaffes] Cleft staffs about three feet long, on which, in the ancient mode of spinning, wool or flax was wound.

122 *Liv.* I warrant ye. *Exeunt.*] Following this line, F1 erroneously inserts a short scene headed, "*Scaena Tertia*", a scene repeated as the conclusion of scene v. MS gives the scene only in the second position, and internal

evidence shows the second position to be correct, since its omission there would provide a scene closing with the exit of Petronius, Petruchio, etc., the next scene opening with their immediate re-entry. F2 and subsequent editors, except Dyce, incorrectly retain the scene as scene iii and omit it in the second position.

II.iii

4 *Row*. So, were] So MS; F1 begins this line "*Row*. Thou hast heard I am sure of Esculapius" and repeats it again in its correct position ten lines later. Professor Bald says in *The Beaumont and Fletcher Folio of 1647*: "The intervening dialogue would undoubtedly have struck Herbert as profane. The suspicion that a cut has been made here is confirmed by the fact that [the second occurrence of the line] has a prefix *Row*., although the previous five lines also belong to Rowland. If one accepts the possibility of a cut one can see at once that a new prefix would have been required here."

14 Esculapius] Roman god of medicine.

21 rack] Cloud.

24 Spur-gald] A horse, etc., chafed or galled with the spur in riding.

33 Tell her . . . for loves sake – – – –] Following this line MS inserts line 36, "Our old love and our friend-ship", leaves blank space enough for about six lines, and continues exactly as in F1-2 but omits line 36 where it occurs in F1-2. Professor Bald feels that the six-line space indicates that the lines of MS copy-text were scored out too heavily for the scribe to read and that he left the space to be filled in later from what he might be able to decipher from the deleted passage or from another source.

43 cold i'th mouth] I.e., dead.

II.iv

8 stiffe] Stubborn; unyielding.

16 Spindle] An allusion to the Fates who spun, measured, and cut man's thread of life.

17 Nell a Greece] Helen.

18 the wise Saylors wife] Penelope, the wife of Ulysses (Mason).

20 ride the wild Mare] A mare was a wooden frame on which soldiers were made to ride for punishment.

21 tabor] Beat as upon a drum.

29 flock-bed] A bed stuffed with the coarse tufts and refuse of wool or cotton, or of cloth torn to pieces.

31 She shall be pamperd with‑ ‑ ‑] MS reads "with,", but there is the possibility, as Dyce points out, that some obscene word has been deleted.

41 Sturbridge Faire] The annual fair kept in the neighborhood of Cambridge (Dyce).

49-50 They are genealogy of Jennets, gotten
And born thus, by the boysterous breath of husbands;] The Spanish jennet engendered by the wind is a favourite fiction in romance; thus in *Rule a Wife and Have a Wife*, "Do you conceive, as our jennets do, with a west wind?" IV.iii.77 (Weber).

51 sure] Steadfastly.

52 favours] Ribbons or scarfs given as tokens of affection.

56 main] Heavy or large.

57 dart ladles] I.e., throw ladles.
tossing irons] MS, F1-2 agree on "tossing", but Sympson suggested "toasting", and Colman so emended. Mason said that "tossing" was not an epithet but a participle of the verb to toss; Weber says that tossing may mean sharp, and Dyce holds that tossing irons may be pokers.

60 Emperious Codsheads] I.e., imperious Godsheads; sovereign divinity.

63 Against the soveraigne peace of Puritans] "The rage of the Puritans against these harmless sports has been ridiculed by Fletcher in another place, more at length and with strong humour, (Women Pleased, IV.i)"

(Weber).

64 Morris] A grotesque dance performed by persons in fancy costume, usually representing characters from the Robin Hood legend – hence, any similar mumming performance.

64 maugre] In spite of.

65 Dudgeon-daggers] A dagger with a haft made out of a certain type of wood called dudgeon (probably box-wood).

73 quarter-sessions] A court held four times a year and usually presided over by a justice of the peace.

84 Metheglin] A spiced or medicated form of mead, originally peculiar to Wales.

91 washing beetle] "A rammer, or batting staff, used by laundresses to press the linen in washing" (Weber).

92 something Ile doe; but what it is I know not.] J. Nichols in 1778 edition calls attention to *Lear*, II.iv 283-4: "– –I will do such things – – what they are, yet I know not!"

II.v

Scaena quinta. . . .] See note II.ii.122.

2 strength] Strong-hold –Dyce.

II.vi

2 carted] Usually associated with bawds and whores who were carried about the streets in a cart as a punishment.

14 horn mad] Furious; stark mad.

15 *Sicely*] A form of the first name "Cicely" (and so Dyce spells it) and must refer to some kind of "gentle" woman or simple girl as opposed to Petruchio's first wife.

17 Pinck] A small flat-bottomed ship having bulging sides; sometimes warships.

Foyst] A barge; perhaps the Lord Mayor's painted barge.

Cockle-boat] A small boat for fishing cockles.

18 To hang her Fights out] To hang cloths about the deck

to conceal combatants on shipboard.

19 equal] Just.

35 flaunt] Action of making a display.

36 stick of Fiddles, and they firke] The ostensible meaning is that the women have music and that they are dancing; the suggestive undertones, however, are hard to ignore.

40 And bid the Kingdom kisse 'em] The women have tucked up their coat-tails and are telling the world to kiss their bare behinds.

42 Tyrants] Weber says that this refers to the ranting of Herod and other despots in the old morality plays.

43 Lansket] So MS, F1-2; this word has eluded all editors; Dyce suggested a lancet window, but this hardly seems likely since all texts read "loose lansket" and a lancet window could hardly be loose. LMS and UIMS read "keyhole" which indicates that they were not familiar with "lansket" or chose to substitute a more common word.

44 *SONG . . . .*] This song is difficult to place in the dialogue; see historical collation.

62 drunk] So F1 and MS. F2 reads "drank" and all subsequent editors, except Dyce, have used the incorrect form "drank".

75 let] I.e., stand in the way of.

81 three pil'd] Of highest quality.

82 Bob-tailes] Contemptible fellows.

86 sack] White wine imported from Spain or the Canaries.

94 *Tom Tilers*] A hen-pecked husband; "The allusion is to an early drama called *Tom Tyler and his Wife*, in which the lady lords it over her husband" (Dyce).

97 Ere I goe lesse] "I.e., before I put up with worse conditions" (Weber).

104 recreant] So MS. MS first read "recant" but this was crossed out and "recreant" added in another hand. Mason suggests that the F1-2 reading "recant" should be emended to "recreant" since the lines following it list the punishments of recreant knights; earlier Pe-

truchio says, "We will beleaguer 'em, and either starve
'em out, / Or make 'em recreant." I.iii.276. Dyce calls
attention to another parallel where Maria says, "If we
beleeve, and you prove recreant *Livia*", II.ii.78.

106 chambring] Sexual indulgence. "Let us walk honestly,
. . . not in chambering and wantonness . . . *Rom.* 13, 13.

112-113 videlicet our Plackets / Let Laces hang] That is to say,
let the openings in our petticoats be unlaced.

131 Apothecaries] "I suppose at Apothecaries' Hall"
(Weber). It seems probable, however, that just an
apothecary's is meant.

156-157 Tis not now / As when Andrea liv'd] A quotation from
Kyd's *The Spanish Tragedy* III.xiii.11. (Dyce).

III.i

9 misereri's] This correction was first suggested by
Sympson; it restores the meter and could have easily
been misread to give MS and F2 "Mistresses" or F1
"miseries". Sympson called attention to V.ii.1. 25-27:
"The two Fish-streets
Were she but once ariv'd amongst the Whitings,
Would sing a wofull *misereri Pedro*."
Colman, however, was the first editor to alter the text.

14 firke] Beat. "Our authors are remarkably fond of this
word with its various meanings." See note II.iv.36.

30 Fryppery] An old clothes shop.

32 rose] An ornamental knot of ribbon worn on shoes, etc.
swabber] A mop or a swab.

33-34 If thou canst love so neer to keep thy making, /
Yet thou wilt loose thy language.]
"That is, if you can love so prudently and thriftily as to
preserve thy making, yet thou wilt lose thy language"
(Mason).
"Making" here means independence or sovereignty.

39 cant] Whine like a beggar; beg.

50-57 *Tran.* Of what religion . . . and that end,] This long
anti-Catholic speech, found only in MS, would have
most certainly been objectionable to a censor.

65 Kits] Small fiddles used by dancing masters.

82-83 now will I erect / A new Game and go hate for th'bell]
Weber says that this may mean, through allusion to
"bear the bell", that Rowland is going to attempt to
be the foremost of woman haters.

87 stinted] Stopped; i.e., he has run out of money.

III.ii

25 Bragget] A drink made of honey and ale fermented
together.

28 Landskip] I.e., landscape.

29 Posset] A drink made of hot milk curdled with liquor.

30 Tumbrel] A flat bottomed boat or barge. See III.v.121.
Dutch hoy] A small Dutch sailing vessel rigged like a
sloop and used for hauling goods short distances.

31 ballasse] I.e., Balance.

33 simperd] Smiled in a silly, self-conscious, or affected
manner.

34 striker] Fornicator.

37 Harry-groat] "This groat, which was struck in the time
of Henry VIII., bears the head of the king, with a long
face and long hair" (Weber).

43 *Cinque-a-pace*] A lively dance, identified with the *gal-
liard*; the steps were regulated by the number five; here,
probably a nickname for a "fast" woman.

44 Tost and Butter] A woman fond of eating; cf., Shakespeare's *Henry IV, Part I*, II.ii.125 where Poins says
in referring to Falstaff. "Wat says Sir John Sack and
Sugar."
had her Bob to?] I.e., had her trick too?

45 filching] Stealing.

46. offer at a Spoon] Start or try to steal a spoon.

III.iii

4 stud] A collection; alluding to a collection of mares
kept for breeding purposes.

11 washt an Ethiope] I.e., to wash an Ethiopian until he

is white; to attempt the impossible.

18 quit] I.e., requite.

20 little ones] I.e., little oaths.

26 huntes-up] Originally an early morning song played to awaken hunters; hence a disturbance or uproar.

39 light] Easy to accomplish.

45 verjuce] The juice of sour fruit.

48 begger's both] I.e., to make both of us beggars.

49 She shall be] I.e., she shall be a beggar.
   Doxy] A beggar's trull; a prostitute.

53 purffle] A border of embroidery.

55 state] Estate.

57 bespeak] Order.

58 civill] Solemn, grave, sober.

66 Ten cast of Hawkes] Ten couple of hawks.
   For th'River] I.e., for the sport of hawking.

71 run a tilt] Compete as a combatant in the lists.

75 morals] Meanings.

80 tild fog] I.e., a fog with a roof on it.
   Lodge] Arbor.

85 And i'th] Scribe of MS began this line by repeating line 83, "What if I pluck it down" and then realizing his error marked out this incorrect beginning.

91 battel'd] I.e., fortified.

98 sumpters] Packs or saddle-bags.

119 he's sooner fire then powder] I.e., he turns to fire quicker than gunpowder.

157 rare breakfast] MS has the variant spelling "reare". It is difficult not to imagine a pun is intended here.

159 Tom o'Lincoln] Professor Maxwell points out that the present great bell of Lincoln cathedral dates from 1855 but that it was preceded by two earlier, great bells. The first, which hung during the time of Queen Elizabeth, was recast in the latter part of 1610, was "christened 'Great Tom of Lincoln' and was rung on Sunday, January 27, 1611". This topical allusion helps Professor Maxwell date the *Woman's Prize* in 1611.

165 worry] Seize by the throat with the teeth.
171 neer it] I.e., near to making her a rascal.

III.iv

9 haire] I.e., the hair in the locket attached to the chain.
21 puppy] A coxcomb; a simpleton.
51 Angels] Gold coins having the device of the archangel
Michael and the dragon, and worth about 10s. each.
56 in good hand] Under control.

III.v

4 die, didle, didle die] "These words are probably the
ridiculous burden of some obsolete ballad" (Weber).
7 Aquavite] Any form of ardent spirits taken as a drink.
10 Bush] Probably, the name of a tavern.
33 Hath sent a watch by this time] "Whenever the plague
was known to rage in a house, the city-officers placed
a guard before the door to prevent any one entering it
during a period of forty days" (Weber).
54 gentlemen] So MS; om. F1 *; its restoration to the text
completes an otherwise short line.
55-64 If any man misdoubt me . . . Velvet costard] MS omits
these lines; in addition MS eliminates 70 S.D.-72 "Exit
Doctor . . . is but one way," and substitutes: "Petro.
fetch a Doctor presently, / and if he can doe no good
on him, he must to Bedlam." Thus MS omits the Doctor
and Pothecary altogether. Bald (Bibliographical Studies
in the Beaumont & Fletcher Folio of 1647) says that
on first sight it would seem "possible that the episode
. . . was added on revision by Fletcher", but there is
also the possibility that MS represents a text used by
a company with limited resources on tour in the country.
62 ounces] I.e., ounces of blood.
63 Deuz-ace] In dice, bad luck; a general term of contempt.
64 Velvet] I.e., the velvet hat worn by physicians.
costard] apple head; a term of contempt.

close-stoole] A chamber pot enclosed in a box or stool.

72 tokens] Spots on the body indicating the plague.

84-85 The blessing of her grandam Eve light on her, /
Nothing but thin fig leaves to hide her knavery.]
So MS; om. F1 *; this speech was probably censored
for being bawdy.

90 onions] Cooked onions were commonly used as a
poultice.

96 state] Estate.

100 chain-bullets] A devastating charge of bullets chained
together and fired from a cannon. Such a charge was
particularly effective in destroying the rigging of an
enemy ship.

103 Have among ye] To go at or get at, esp. in a hostile
way; it announces the speaker's intention to get at or
attack.

105 crackers] I.e., fireworks; firecrackers.

106 *Green-sleeves*] An allusion to an old ballad of the same
name, concerning an inconstant lady.

111 doubles] A sharp turn in running, as of a hunted hare.

116 Quartern-ague] I.e., a fourth of a pestilent fever—one
that never kills but is continuously annoying.

121 tith] Tight.
Tumbrell] See III.ii.30.

124 hedge-hogs] An animal armed with spines; also applied
to persons who are inconsiderate of others' feelings.
againe] So MS. F1-2 complete this line: "I could rail
twenty daies;" in respect to this Colman says: "We
think it cannot be doubted but that the words *I could
rail twenty days*, have been foisted in here by mistake,
and have therefore omitted them. They come in their
proper place afterwards lower down, where the line runs,
    I could rail twenty days together now.
There they complete the measure; here they interrupt
it, as well as break in upon the sense."

131 stringing of the Fiddles] Sexual activity.

132 suffer'd] Permitted.

136 leap] Copulate.

137-138 they are said to kill / With kindnesse] Oliphant says that this speech is a "glance at Heywood's *Woman Killed with Kindness* (1603).

140 in old wals with their heeles upward] I.e., in old graves face downward.

144 go a birding] Go shooting birds – the birds here being the women.

IV.i

6 whim-wham] Trifle; trinket.

7 Jib-crack] Trifle; knick-knack.

Gentleman o'th first house] An upstart gentleman (Dyce).

11 busse] Kiss.

15 bobs] Tricks.

16 quillets] Verbal niceties or subtle distinctions.

19 a sow of Lead] An ingot of lead.

Quoat] Make a note of.

31 fond] Foolish.

32 the Ballad, crabbed age] Reed's note in Colman's edition calls attention to a poem printed in *The Passionate Pilgrim* and attributed to Shakespeare:

"Crabbed age and youth cannot live together:
Youth is full of pleasance, age is full of care;
. . . ."

33 *May* and *Ianuary*] "Refers to the Merchant's Tale of Chaucer" (Weber).

42 Owches] Clasps, buckles, or brooches.

44 Cals] I.e., cauls; a netted cap worn by women; a net for the hair.

48 an order bore my nostrils] I.e., another takes my place; Moroso is concerned about Rowland's position with Livia.

53 tricks] Habits; ways of acting.

54 forerunners of the ancient measures] Announcers of old standards or ideas; "measures" probably means dances.

55 Verdugoes] Hangman's (Nares).

59 lavish] Unrestrained; loose; licentious.

107 posset] See note III.ii.29.

IV.ii

4 march Beere] A strong, dark beer or ale usually brewed in March.

5 Rundlets] Small barrels.

8 batter brawne] Drink with roast pig.

17 But while she shewes all these, and all their losses] "That is, while she shews all these bad qualities, and at the same time the want of them all" (Mason).

18 linsey woolsey] From the name of a kind of cloth, a strange medley of contradictions.

23 colour] A show of reason.

32 pet] Offence at being slighted or not made enough of.

48 debosh'd companion] Debauch'd fellow (Weber).

51 Keeper . . . of fourescore] An eighty-year-old woman.

52-53 mew'd content / And all her teeth together] I.e., the old woman had lost (mew'd or moulted) pleasure and satisfaction in life along with all her teeth (Weber).

85 Grasier] I.e., grazier; one who feeds cattle for the market.

88 dog-leech] A veterinary surgeon who treats dogs; a quack.

91 *Harry* Groats] See III.ii.29.

100 forsweare] swear falsely.

103 lewdest] Most ignorant, bungling, or ill-mannered.

110 Fruiterer] Fruit peddlar; the allusion here is to Eve and the forbidden fruit.

113 sword of veng'ance, with a thred hung o're us] An allusion to the sword of Damocles.

116 *cap a pe*] I.e., *cap-a-pie*; from head to foot.

132 Tit of ten pence] A cheap prostitute – a tit being a base woman or a hussy.

135 bezel'd] Embezzled; stolen.

158 Saying my Prayers back-ward] See II.ii.99.

IV.iii

4 constru'd] Translated.

5 and peirc'd too] As Colman points out, a loose pun is
   certainly intended here.

9 if we crosse it not] If we don't prevent it.

10 see the Papers of one size] I.e., see that the papers
   appear identical in order to manipulate the outcome.

17 Carrick] A large ship of burden.

20 split] I.e., suffer, but the context makes the word in-
   decent.

31 At half sword] Half a swords' length–thus, close together.

IV.iv

13 o'th sullens] A state of gloomy ill-humor.

18 blew bottle] "In allusion to the dress of servants, who
   in ancient times were generally habited in blue" (Weber).

26 toyle] A trap or snare for wild beasts.

27 woodman] Hunter.

29 goes lesse] Plays for a smaller stake; see II.vi.97.

32 affect her] I.e., love her (Weber).

42 I'le no by-blowes] I.e., I'll not hit to the side; I'll come
   straight to the point.

48 Jack o' Lent] "a puppet at which boys in the Lent
   season threw cudgels" (Weber).

49 untag'd points and Compters] Things of little value –
   untagged points are laces without the metal ends;
   compters are imitation coins.

IV.v

28 certaine] Steadfast.

32 Balderdash] A jumbled mixture of liquors.

33 carded] Mixed (Weber).

47 one of those that multiply i'th Suburbs] A prostitute;
   Weber points out that prostitutes were officially con-
   fined to the outskirts of the city.

50 begins her compasse with her fingers] I.e., begins a
circular motion with her hand and indicates the amount
she wants by holding up her fingers.

76 dogged] Surly; sullenly obstinate.

78 tatle] Talk without reticence so as to reveal private
affairs.

89 mumping] Mumbling.

92 trouble] I.e., vexation (Colman).

97 a possession] A state of being possessed by a devil
(Mason).

98 if not more] I.e., at least one devil if not more (Mason).

105 lewd] Ignorant; wicked.

117 point] A ribbon used as a suspender to hold up the
hose.

129 infects our uses] Corrupts our nature or habit.

134 Make but this woman all thy wonders] An allusion to
the many accounts of scientific phenomena Pliny records
in his *Historia Naturalis*.

170 squard] Transformed for the better.
sot] Foolish person.

175-176 what she do's with one i'th day, i'th night / Undoe it
with an other] Penelope knitted by day and unraveled
by night.

194 Cataya] China.

201 canst] I.e., cannot.

228 *Stilo novo*] In the new style; thus "alluding to the
manner in which foreign letters were dated' (Reed–
Colman).

V.i

12 Observing] Heeding.

22 whole] A pun on "hole" is most likely intended here.

35 crop sick] Sick to the stomach.

44 To look gay babies in your eyes] Weber gives the following explanation: "This conceit, which seems to be
founded in the reflection, which really appears in the
iris, of the person placed before it, was a great favourite

in the seventeenth century, and has lately been revived
by a modern rhymester, distinguished for having done
what he could to debase the taste and vitiate the morals
of the 19th century, by the polluted effeminacy of his
writings."
It is likely that Weber is referring to a poem by Thomas
Moore entitled "Impromptu".

> Look in my eyes, my blushing fair.
> Thou'lt see thyself reflected there
> And as I gaze in thine, I see
> Too little miniatures of me
> Thus in our looks some propagation lies,
> For we make babies in each other's eyes.

47 busse] Kiss.

64 teatish] I.e., peevish, and so MS.

67 an hundred] I.e., a hundred pounds of the wager he
made with Tranio.

68 as I pist it] Just as if I had pissed it.
S.D. *Enter Livia discovered abed, and Moroso by her.*]
Professor Bald (see note III.v.55-64) suggests that MS
reading of "in a chaire" for "*abed*" indicates that MS
may represent a touring company's text. Weber points
out that it is not to be supposed that Moroso lay in the
bed with Livia.

69 draw 'em] MS reads "beare her", and Sympson, Colman, and Weber altered the text to read "draw her";
Dyce, however, thinks it strange that the previous
editors "should not have perceived that 'em' meant the
curtains".

72 lightsommer] More cheerful.

79 harrow] There are probably bawdy implications here
since a harrow does not plow but is drawn over a
plowed field to smooth it out; in the next line Livia
says, "That must be drawn to all he dos."

84 Sculler] One who propels a barge or boat by an oar
attached to the stern.

87 Chamblet] I.e., camblet; a costly eastern fabric.

93 casting Bottle] A vinaigrette; a small ornamented bottle with a perforated lid and filled with smelling salts or perfume.

94 toad-stone] A stone supposedly found in the head of a toad and valued as a fettish.

96 translated] Transported out of his senses.

132 meere] Absolute.

Pomander] A mixture of aromatic substances made into a ball and carried as a safeguard against infection.

148 To th' booke sonne.] Mason: "The book means the deed they were to sign. So Glendower says, in the First Part of Henry the Fourth –

'By this our book is drawn, we will but seal,
And then to horse immediately.'

The book here means the instrument by which Glendower, Percy, and Mortimer, shared the kingdom amongst them."

163 quit] Recompense.

V.ii

8-9 as far as Amiens / she'll carry blank] I.e., she will be able to hit us as far away as Amiens. See note I.iii.93.

26 Whitings] Small fish with pearly white flesh and highly esteemed as food.

28 poor *John*] Salted and dried hake.

29 Sea-breach] "I.e., breaking in of the sea" (Dyce).

38 lickrish] Lustful.

47 The grief of her—] "his grief occasioned by her" (Colman).

56 And all his friends to curse her] I.e., and tell all his friends to curse her.

64 *ipso facto*] By that very fact.

fadings] A licentious dance; the implication here is that the man who gives her remedy may not be able to perform this dance.

67-68 A sedgly curse light on him, which is, *Pedro*; / The feind ride through him booted, and spurd, with a

Sythe at's back.] This curse seems to have been a fairly common imprecation and is glossed in *Webster's New International Dictionary*, 2nd ed. Weber quotes Francis Grose's "Proverbs" as saying, and correctly so, that Sedgley is near Dudley in Staffordshire.

V.iii

9 A Contract] I.e., a marriage contract.
34 Let's remove our places.] J. Nichols in Colman's edition (1778) recalls a parallel in *Hamlet*, "where (on account of the ghost calling under the stage) the prince and his friends two or three times remove their situations".
39 Testers] Sixpences.

V.iv

18 defend] Forbid; prohibit.
66 morris] Morris-dance.

EPILOGUE] See note on Prologue.

STUDIES IN ENGLISH LITERATURE

Out:

MOUTON & CO. — PUBLISHERS — THE HAGUE